TREASURES

The Memoir of an Artist

Elaine Marinoff Good

Treasures: The Memoir of An Artist, Published June, 2019
Editorial and proofreading services: Beth Raps, Karen Grennan
Interior layout and cover design: Howard Johnson
Photo Credits: All photos are the sole ownership of Elaine Marinoff Good
Cover Image: *Repose* by Elaine Marinoff, 60″ x 48″, oil on canvas, 1981

Published by SDP Publishing, an imprint of SDP Publishing Solutions, LLC.

The children of Elaine Marinoff Good are committed to publishing her memoir as she intended. In that spirit, we are proud to present this book to readers; however, the story, the experiences, and the words are the author's alone. The contents in this book do not necessarily reflect the views of the publisher nor her surviving children.

ISBN-13 (hardcover): 978-1-7327933-4-7
ISBN-13 (paperback): 978-1-7327933-3-0
ISBN-13 (ebook): 978-1-7327933-5-4
Library of Congress Control Number: 2019938523

Printed in the United States of America

"A vivid memoir of a remarkable woman who came of age during a tumultuous time of transition for women. Her honesty, passion, and humor bond us to this fearless seeker."

—Laura Stein

"Powerful memoir transcends the particular story of a life and connects us with universal truths. The story of a brave woman who breaks free of the conventions of her time and discovers herself in the process."

—Suzette Mullen

"*Treasures* is a memoir of a woman who broke out as an artist against social and artistic constraints. And she does not shade the truth in telling her story."

—Robert Stuart

"Elaine Marinoff was a feminist before she knew the word. Her poignant and inspiring memoir takes the reader on a journey from the California coast to the New York art scene."

—Lynn Blumenfeld

"Crossing the brink of revelation at various intervals in her life and career, Ms. Marinoff demonstrates time and again her ingenuity, courage, and singular vision."

—Stacey Donovan

"Elaine was an adventurous, beautiful soul whose life story is captivating. She is the definition of female individualism. I only wish I had met her when I was younger."

—Nitchie Zunis

Acknowledgments

With gratitude to:

The Ashawagh Hall Writers Workshop.

Eileen Obser, editor. Patricia Carson, assistant.

And Krissy, the office mate.

Table of Contents

CHAPTER

1

Dancing to My Easel

I escaped to my small studio in Venice, California. A sharp southern light streamed in through high, horizontal windows as I passed the welcoming madras daybed. On my small steel desk, I jotted newly sensed longings in a leather journal, put on my paint-spattered lab coat, squeezed oil pigments onto my palette, and painted with frenzy. An artist's work should reflect her life and mine was, for the first time, mired in desire. It was as though I had been asleep, suddenly awakened as this highly charged sexual being. After all those years of deprivation, silence and loneliness, I was on my own . . . a wild animal in heat. Shoving a cassette into the tape deck, I danced to my easel and attacked the canvas. The works that evolved were my most profound, my Erotic Series.

Away from the studio I began wearing long, clingy knit dresses and dyed my black hair red. My friends stopped inviting me and kept silent when they saw me at functions. I felt I had become a fallen woman in their eyes. They were all married. Was I now a threat? Were they jealous?

When I moved to New York in 1988, nine years later, I left those infamous paintings parked in my Venice studio racks and then, when I bought an old factory in Tribeca, I hid them in my basement. They were my hidden past; no one in my new life could have guessed.

CHAPTER

2

Wedded Bliss

The day my new husband Bob Good dissected his first cadaver, he came home smelling of formaldehyde and practiced naming the internal organs of the body on me, as I lay naked on the bed in our small apartment in Los Angeles. I thought marriage was the answer to all of life's problems. Our common goal was to make Bob a doctor. I loved being part of a team and was happier than I ever imagined possible.

His stress level seemed to escalate daily as we settled into domesticity, manifesting itself through his increased smoking. The cause, I presumed, was the fierce competition at school. He knew he had to work extra hard to compete with kids from highly educated, advantaged backgrounds.

We had been married four months when early one morning, Bob popped into our small kitchen, lit a cigarette, and placed it on the edge of the yellow tile sink. He ignited the burner to boil water for coffee and left the room to take a quick shower. Dripping wet, towel wrapped around his waist, he came back to take a puff, and yelled, "Elaine, where's my cigarette?"

"I put it out."

"You what?"

"I thought you forgot it."

"If you ever touch my cigarettes again," he shouted, "so help me, I'm out of here."

A streak of fear shot through me. I stepped into the shower, letting the hot water calm me, then dressed in silence and drove him to school on my way to work. I hurried to clock in at J.J. Haggarty's, a women's specialty store in Beverly Hills; rode up the elevator to the ad department and sat at my layout and paste-up table as though nothing had changed. The ads and direct mails had to go out, and I needed the job. We were living on what I earned.

At the end of the day I clocked out, but instead of my usual dash, drove slowly west on Wilshire toward the hospital and turned on a classical station to soothe my churning stomach. When I arrived at the UCLA turn-around, Bob was already there, impatiently pacing. He got in, immediately shut my music off and reached into his lab coat pocket for a cigarette, lit it, and leaning back, blew the smoke straight up toward the roof of the car.

"Busy day," he said, "it'll be good to get home." I tried to smile and speak, but the words stuck in my throat and refused to come out.

As I prepared dinner, Bob sat with his scotch and Pall Malls. We ate our meatloaf and mashed potatoes as I listened to his day's events, then he went into the bedroom to study. I did the dishes, then silently got out the old sewing machine from my dress-making days to continue putting together the living room drapes.

We met in our last year of college in Dr. Garfinkel's Social Disorganization class. I had just transferred to UCLA from Cal Berkeley. A dark-haired fellow with perfect features motioned me over with his eyes. I plunked my books down on the desk and slipped into the seat next to him. After that initial day we often studied together, and I came to realize that Bob had a brilliant mind, was sensitive, idealistic and different than the other boys

I had dated. He wanted to heal the world. Being a doctor was his dream; mine was marriage and a family.

When he came to my house during our courtship, my father would call up to me, "Elaine, your breath of sunshine is here," and I would shyly come down the staircase, take his hand, and we'd be on our way in his creamy 1950 Ford coupe. He was everything, and we fell in love. Our dating lasted a year, culminating with Kappa Sigma serenading as I accepted his fraternity pin.

On the 9th of June, 1957, smoldering gray clouds threatened rain as our wedding was taking place in my parents' small back yard. In his rented white tux jacket and black pants with a silk stripe up the sides, Bob had a pasted-on nervous grin during the entire afternoon. I could feel his knees shake as we danced, tripping over the train of my white organdy gown, as the combo serenaded and the singer imitated Frank Sinatra.

We were both twenty-two and frightened, but marriage was what we did in the fifties after college; it was expected. After we cut the cake and stuffed it into each others' mouths for the photo shoot, he gently put his arm around my waist and whispered, "Can we get out of here? I'm suffocating." I wanted to stay, but could see he was desperate, and I did not know how to say no.

We ran down the wide brick steps as the crowd threw rice. Cans clinked on the road, tied to the back fender of the new blue and white Ford, a gift from my parents. We drove three blocks and stopped to take them off. I blurted out, "I want to go back; everyone we care about is in that house." But we were on our way, and there was no turning back.

Medical school was his obsession. But at the end of his third year, after being exhausted from studying and smoking all night, he said, "I've got to get away or I'll crack." The next day, he mentioned that he was thinking about dropping out of school. I was determined not to let him do it. Summer was approaching, and I felt it was crucial that we go on a trip. He was physically and emotionally collapsing. In Haggarty's drab, gray executive office on the third floor, I waited for the supervisor to beg my case. I had been there two years with no vacation, and hesitantly sputtered out my need for time off with pay.

With her white hair piled high on her head, wearing a maroon skirted suit and matching pumps, she reached out, and put her hands on my shoulders. "My dear, I'm so sorry, that's impossible. We're starting a huge promotion next month. Direct mails and ads will be flying out of here. We can't do without your position, and so many are waiting in line for your job."

So, in spite of needing the income, I reluctantly quit, worrying how we would survive. Could I get another job?

We drove south to the Mexican border, wound our way around to the interior of Sonora, turned on the radio and, looking at each other, burst out laughing. Nat King Cole was singing "That Lucky Old Sun" and we joined in. Bob's cigarettes stayed in his pocket. The farther away from UCLA we drove, the more relaxed he became. We stopped in Hermosillo and ended up in Taxco, a quaint silver mining village nestled in the hills. We checked into the old colonial Hotel Victoria and walked hand in hand through the village, stopping to rest in the massive Santa Prisca de Taxco.

In one of the silversmith shops, I admired a shiny angular ring. Bob said, "Come on, let's try it on for size." The sales girl pulled it out from the window display and placed it on my index finger.

"We can't afford this, Bob," I said, as he dragged the salesgirl to the corner, then came back smiling.

"It's yours!"

I reached up and gave him a big hug as he glowed and whispered in my ear. "It was under a dollar."

We stuffed ourselves on homemade tamales and enchiladas, and later went back to our tiny lavender-colored room overlooking the small village.

When we returned home, I found a new job at Rose Marie Reid Swimsuit Company, doing essentially the same work, plus taking models on photo shoots and showing the new fashion line to ladies' charity groups. I received double the pay and relished the glamour.

Three months after our trip, I had not gotten my period and was beginning to show. The gynecologist confirmed my suspicion. Wanting to surprise Bob that night with the news, I bought a bottle of cheap champagne and made chocolate chip cookies, his favorite. We had eaten dinner and were enjoying the champagne. As he munched on a cookie, I said, "You know the day we hiked up the mountain in Taxco? When we returned, and church bells chimed as we made love in the Hotel Victoria, with the orange bougainvillea climbing its walls?" He flashed a broad smile, reached his arm out and pulled me close.

"I think that's when we conceived . . . "

There was a long silence. "You're serious?"

"I saw the doctor today. I'm pregnant."

His face turned ashen. I yearned for some token of affection or simply: *Sweetheart, that's wonderful, a little baby on the way, our child*. Instead, he stood there, glaring at me with a blank expression.

Wearing only a T-shirt and gray shorts, he nervously took out a cigarette. He looked away as he lit it and, without saying a word, inched his way over to the door and walked out.

I washed the dishes, put on my nightgown and robe, dragged one of our wicker dining chairs out onto our narrow wood slat deck, and poured myself a glass of the champagne. When my glass was empty, I brought the bottle out and sat in the cold November dark, waiting for him to return.

After drinking the rest of the bottle, I hobbled into bed and passed out. It must have been three or four in the morning when I smelled the odor of stale tobacco and felt his body close, his heavy arm wrapped around my back.

My svelte figure became thick as the months progressed, and after my sixth month, I could hide it no longer. It was embarrassing, in my new glamorous job, and I anxiously waited each day to get the ax. Finally, as expected, I was summoned to the main office of Rose Marie Reid, where a committee of senior personnel greeted me, stone-faced, as if I had committed a crime. They told me I was fired for being pregnant. I accepted it without complaint, said "I'm sorry for disappointing you," thanked them, and walked directly into the ladies' bathroom, shaking, and vomited. It was 1960.

We never considered asking for financial help. His family could not afford it, and although my parents liked Bob, they were initially against the marriage because of our differing religious backgrounds. I knew they only wanted my happiness, but we were determined to make it on our own and too proud to give them the satisfaction of saying, "I told you so."

Wearing my Aunt Pearl's hand-me-down maternity clothes, I waited in the West Los Angeles Board of Equalization unemployment line each week, with the homeless and jobless, until our beautiful baby girl, Cindy, was born on the 25th of May 1960, and afterwards, until the benefits ran out. Bob stood in other lines to sell his blood and sperm. He often brought home baloney from the ten o'clock snack at the hospital in a paper towel, and we would eat it the next night for dinner.

The birth took place two weeks before Bob's graduation. My parents stayed with little Cindy while I went to the ceremony. It was my first time out since Cindy's arrival, and that day, sitting amongst the other wives and families wearing hats and fineries in the June sunshine, I was so proud to be a part of his journey. When he received his degree, as Bob reached the podium, I could see him searching the audience for me. When he saw me in the second row, his eyes lit up, and then the provost announced:

"To Robert Glen Good, I present this degree, Doctor of Medicine . . . and congratulations, you are this year's recipient of the Summa Cum Laude award." He graduated first in his class.

Two weeks later, in the morning mist of mid-June, the sun beginning to show its magical light, five new, young medical doctors piled into the crimson Chevy of the only woman in their graduating class. Their destination was San Francisco for State Board exams. Bob hugged me good-bye, walked down the stairs, then surprised me by coming back up the two flights to hug little Cindy and kiss me again.

"Forgot to do this," he said. "See you both in three days." I thought, *Three long days and nights alone with the baby. Can I manage without Bob nearby?* The next day I walked into Westwood Village with Cindy in the stroller and sat in the sunshine, drinking coffee. Bob called that night from a pay phone to tell me the exams were tougher than he predicted. The following night, I drove over to my parents' for dinner after waiting hours in the unemployment line with the fussing baby. On the third day, I sat with Cindy on the balcony at twilight, watching the sun go down and the moon come up, waiting for him. I thought, *perhaps the exams have gone on longer than expected.* The next day, I stayed home, expecting him all day, but he did not come or call. That night I started to panic, and called the police. *Maybe they got into an accident.* I described the car and route they were taking; the police assured me that no incident had occurred involving that description.

I called the wife of one member of the group. She put me on with her husband. "We decided to fly back. Bob's driving with Janice; he should be home soon."

By day five I still had not heard from him. What if something happened to the baby? I became frightened. On the sixth day, I was bathing Cindy when the front door sprung open at around noon, surprising me. Bob's face was flushed. I wrapped the baby in a soft yellow towel, and we went into the living room. The baby and I were nestled together, trying to hug him, to show how happy we were to have him back. I noticed he was stammering, standoffish, his eyes avoiding mine; he could not get the words out.

"We came back along Highway One," he said, "stopped in Carmel. Such a beautiful drive."

"I know, we were there on our honeymoon, remember?"

He said it was late and motels were expensive. They shared a room, and one thing led to another. "You know how it is."

"You shared a room with Janice? Janice Kayahara? No, I don't know how it is."

I was numb as his confession sank in. I had the feeling that by admitting his betrayal, he imagined honesty would make up for his guilt. In a state of disbelief, stabbed in my gut, I could not look at or go near him. I spent the night holding Cindy on the living room couch while Bob slept soundly in the bed.

The next day, the bell rang in the apartment at noon. I opened the door, my long hair uncombed and my eyes bloodshot, wearing a red wrap robe with a Japanese dragon on the back. Holding the baby in my arms, I looked out and said, "Excuse me, do I know you?"

"I'm Janice Kayahara, from the medical school, remember? Wanted to give little Cindy a gift." Bob peeked out from the bedroom in shock.

Janice stood there reeking of cologne, her blouse tight and skirt short, with a fancy haircut. *It had been so long since I had a professional cut.* She handed me a present all wrapped in pink, with a flowered sleeper for the baby inside. Before I knew it, Bob was ushering her in, offering her coffee.

I put the baby in her bassinet, stepped into the bathroom to comb my hair, grabbed Bob's shirt off the hook from last night and put on his gray shorts. *Good grief, what's she doing here?* My hands trembled and a blast of pain shot through my head. I walked out holding my breath, needing to get rid of her. Sensing my anxiety, the baby started crying and would not stop. When Janice finally walked out the door, I didn't allow myself to admit my treasured husband's participation in the affair.

"How could you let that woman into our home?"

He stood silent, hands clasped together on his chest.

I dumped the flowered sleeper in the trash, prepared formula in bottles, turned on the burner to sterilize, gave him instructions to turn it off in twenty minutes, and placed the baby in his arms as he watched me in silence. He had never held her for more than moments. I took the keys and ran down the stairs.

With no place to go, I drove aimlessly, ending at Malibu Beach amid the June crowds. Down on the sand at the edge of the water, I let the waves wash over my feet. I lingered an hour, then panic set in. The baby was alone with Bob. Did he even know how to burp her? She could aspirate. I ran to the car and raced home amid rush hour traffic, dashing up the two flights of stairs. Out of breath, I marched in.

He had not moved in the two hours I had been gone. The formula was still cooking in the sterilizer; the baby's diaper was wet and full. She was bright red, screaming, and he was helpless, in tears. In my muddled brain, I heard him say, "Sweetheart, I love you and little Cindy so much. I'm sorry, please forgive me."

I gently picked the baby up without a word as Bob's arms reached out to me, took her over to the changing table to clean her up, and went into the bedroom. Sitting in the garage-sale rocker, I unbuttoned my blouse and proceeded to nurse. Bob came in and sat on the edge of the yellow bedspread, blowing his nose. I noticed him checking his watch. Then his glazed eyes glanced at it again. I moved the baby to my other breast. In a few minutes, Bob looked at his wrist again, then abruptly came over and grabbed her away from me.

"What are you doing?"

"The text book says only ten minutes on each side."

"But she's hungry, she's not finished."

He held her away from me and she started screaming. Then he took her to the living room, and put her on the couch, face up. I ran after him.

"Stop, Bob, you're acting crazy."

I lifted Cindy into my arms to burp, holding her very close, and we went back into the bedroom. I shut the door and sat down again, rocking back and forth until my little angel with big brown eyes and masses of dark, silky hair fell asleep. In retrospect, I know he only meant well, but he frightened me so much that I was reluctant to nurse again. How could I question the great doctor? He was now the voice of authority.

CHAPTER

3

Vodka

The hot October Santa Ana winds had died down. Cindy and I sat on the red plaid blanket under the sycamore tree in the UCLA garden, waiting for Bob. His surgical internship was demanding and I missed him terribly. As five-month-old Cindy crawled around, Bob arrived in his white lab coat over a starched blue shirt to take his dinner break with us. I dished out tuna casserole from a Tupperware container as Bob lay down on the blanket, leaning on one elbow, smiling as he watched the baby. I listened as he told me about his day and details of the heart transplant he had observed. He was looking forward to the neurosurgical rotation the following week. Reaching into his lab coat hip pocket, he pulled out a Pall Mall and, lighting it, told me he had dreamed of becoming a neurosurgeon since childhood. I moved closer, took his hand and told him it was good to see him.

"You too," he said, then glanced at his watch, smashed his cigarette out in the grass, kissed each of us on the cheek and said. "Gotta get back. See you guys in the morning."

Holding the baby up, I waved her little hand and said, "Bye, bye, Daddy," as we watched him disappear into the hospital.

Alone on the blanket, I put Cindy on my stomach, holding her up by her hands. We smelled the rose garden as we witnessed the evening sky grow pink through fluttering, golden sycamore leaves fading into the night. "It's just you and me, my sweet."

I propped myself up in bed, reading Truman Capote's *In Cold Blood,* and drank my peppermint tea. Unable to sleep, I ambled into the kitchen searching for something to knock me out. Opening the cupboard above the refrigerator, I saw a half full bottle of Smirnoff vodka and, remembering the night I passed out from champagne, grabbed it. *Maybe this will help.*

I poured the vodka over ice. It was strong and bitter. I added orange juice and, carrying it back to the bedroom, tripped in the dark, spilling it on the living room floor. The baby heard me and started crying. I picked her up, warmed a bottle and fed her. She finally settled down and I went back to the kitchen and poured more vodka, using the rest of the orange juice. In the bedroom again, I sipped as I continued to read. When the words on the page became blurred, I nodded off, awakening with a start as the front door gently closed. Bob was home and it was morning. I dragged myself out of bed, easing up slowly, and glanced in the mirror. I had spilled vodka on my lace nightgown and thought, *Hope he doesn't notice these stains and my bloodshot eyes.*

"Hi, sweetheart," I said, giving him a hug. "Have a hard night?"

"You okay? Don't look so good."

"I'm fine, didn't sleep well. Hungry?" I said, as I picked the book up from the floor, hoping I had not left the bottle out by accident.

Looking over, I saw him walking through the living room to the kitchen.

"Eek! What's this stuff all over the floor? I just fell. What'd you do? Smells like liquor, it's sticky. Better clean it up."

Rushing over, I pulled him up, ran into the bathroom, grabbing a hand towel to mop. "Sorry, an accident. You okay?"

I stuck a slice of whole wheat bread in the toaster. Trying to hide my face behind my long hair, I looked down at Cindy as I fed her.

"Where's my orange juice?"

"Ran out; I'll get more today." He finished eating and, with a scowl, went into the bedroom. I dressed us quickly and took the baby out so he could sleep. With Cindy in the stroller, we walked to Safeway in the village and I grabbed a large bottle of Smirnoff, hiding it under the lettuce and ground beef in case someone I knew came by. When we returned, Bob stepped out of the shower and put on a crisp white shirt, blue-striped tie and lab coat, with four pens neatly placed in his upper left pocket. He enjoyed portraying the image of the well-dressed intern and loved to rush back to the hospital. I patiently waited until he left, then refilled the vodka bottle above the refrigerator and hid the new one in the bottom of the dirty clothes hamper.

The next night he came in, drained and exhausted. We climbed into bed, snuggling together, and he immediately crashed. Entrapped in our cozy warm bed, I watched the perfect features of his handsome face, hair tumbling over his eyes. I yearned to talk, to hear about his day and his world of medicine, but felt like an outsider begging to be let in. I lay there thinking of everything I wanted to say about the baby and our day, not moving, afraid I would wake him. It must have been hours before I finally mustered the courage to get up.

Dangling one foot over the edge of the bed, then the other, I quietly closed the door and tiptoed though the hall and darkened living room into the kitchen. Reaching above the refrigerator to the cabinet, I found the vodka. This time I added less orange juice, craving the bitterness and the oblivion it brought on. The cold liquid trickled down my throat as I sat in a catatonic state. It did not take long for my senses to numb and my loneliness to disappear. When I realized I might pass out, I carefully put the glass in the sink and stumbled back into bed, my absence unnoticed.

Five months later, I was coming in from the village at around 6pm. The baby was hungry and crying; I was wilted. I had seen the neighbors from the building, but they were only faces not formally met. The round-faced fellow from next door in a white shirt, horn-rimmed glasses and a stocky build, called over to me.

"Hi there, haven't seen you around lately. I'm Stewart. How's the new orange couch? I saw them bringing it up."

"At last, a real sofa," I said. "I made the old one and it finally fell apart."

"Want some help up the stairs with the groceries?"

"Sure, I could use your muscle. I'll take the baby."

Without thinking, I invited him in to see the sofa. He carried the stroller over his head, strongman fashion, with the groceries in his other hand.

"Wow, it's bright! Really livens the place up."

"It's all about color; bright colors can change your life. Want a glass of wine? I've got Gallo."

I hardly knew him, but a jumble of words came tumbling out. I changed Cindy's diaper then fed her the bottle, while he sat in the kitchen, watching and listening. Perhaps he was flirting, but I only saw a helpful neighbor witnessing my tales of woe. He told me he had been a psych major in college. I thought, *good training for listening to me,* as I babbled on. He said he was working with a start-up company called Computer Sciences.

We talked about ourselves as he leaned back, arms folded at his waist. I remembered Stewart's wife from the hospital. She was my delivery room nurse. It was so easy to talk with a stranger, and before I knew it, I was sharing details of Bob's affair with Janice. A sudden rush of emotions engulfed me and unleashed a flood of tears I had held back for months. I put the baby down to sleep, and we went into the living room to the orange couch.

"Do you love him? Want to stay?"

"Oh yes, he's my life. I want to be with him until I die. My goal is to make him happy."

"Isn't there something else you've wanted to do with your life?"

"Well, I did want to be an artist when I was a kid. I went to Chouinard Art Institute at sixteen, but in 1950 that wasn't a viable profession, especially for a woman. We didn't even have an art museum in L.A. My folks encouraged me to be a fashion designer since I made all my own clothes."

I told Stewart that between my junior and senior years in college, I studied fashion in Paris. On my way to my *pension* at the end of my second week, I stopped into the Louvre, and sitting in front of the paintings of Tintoretto, Modigliani, Delacroix and the one brave woman, Artemisia Gentileschi, I found solace. It proved to me that being a painter was okay. I told him of my dreams about those paintings and of going back to the Louvre day after day.

"But now I'm a married woman," I said. "My priorities have changed. My husband's my life and if I did work, I'd need to earn real money. Artists are poor. We can't survive on the $90.00 a month Bob's earning as an intern."

"You know that's only temporary. You can't give up your dreams."

That night as I sat alone with my vodka, I could think of nothing but those magnificent paintings in the Louvre and the struggles Artemisia Gentileschi must have endured.

I had not seen Stewart for a week. His back door butted up against ours and I was startled by an unexpected knock on that door. It was Stewart, bubbling over with enthusiasm.

"I've got an idea," he said. "Why don't you take your love of art in another direction and become an interior designer?"

"What? Where did you get that idea?"

"You'd be decorating other people's homes for a fee. You'll need to take some courses, learn the essentials, but you're a natural." He told me that I'd be great, judging by how I had put together and livened up our dreary apartment.

I wrestled with Stewart's idea for days, then put the baby in the stroller and walked over to UCLA's registration office for the Extension schedule. My Aunt Pearl, a successful interior designer, was enthusiastic when I told her Stew's idea. She encouraged me to come with her to search for fabrics for a client.

Petite Pearl Brown, with her cropped black hair and endless compassion, had been my mentor since I was twelve, when she married my mother's brother, Josiah, a medical student. The following week I left the baby with Mother and Aunt Pearl picked me up. We drove to Robertson and Beverly Boulevard, where we waltzed from one decorator showroom to the other. Pearl, in her long pink knit dress and single strand of pearls, was confident and smiling, with me in awe by her side. In each place, she introduced me to the receptionist, then went directly to the fabric racks as I watched her flip through, searching for samples to be checked out and presented to her client for upholstery and drapes.

I had never realized such an abundance of interior design resources were available. I could not wait for my class to begin. The following week Pearl and I went to look at furniture, and by the time my one class started, I was excited and gobbled up every word of instruction.

I must have mentioned our financial situation during the long drives because Pearl called to arrange an appointment to bring several friends to my apartment for art lessons. When the doorbell rang, Pearl, wearing an old shirt of Joe's and faded slacks, was ready to get dirty and introduced me to four professors' wives. After fussing over the baby, they sat at my dining table covered with newspapers. I passed around shirt cardboards, brushes, pastels and watercolors, assigning them to paint the fruit in the bowl.

"Be experimental," I said. "Make up your own colors, that'll make it more creative."

"This is so much fun," said one of the wives. "Sure wish my kids could see me." And, as they left, each one gave me three dollars. In 1960, that was enough cash to buy food for a week.

"Please don't," I said. But they insisted, and I realized none of them really cared about the lesson. Pearl had seen how depressed and broke we were and knew I would never accept charity. The following week they came back for another lesson. Pearl led the pack, telling me how much fun they'd had the previous week, and the enthusiastic responses of their families to the small paintings.

Halfway through the lesson, the front door sprung open and Bob marched in after being on duty 24 hours. He was unshaven, tie slung over his shoulder, with a cigarette hanging out of his mouth, exhausted, and wanting me to serve him breakfast. I introduced him and then excused myself to the ladies. They understood. The place was so small it was impossible to carry on with the class, and they pattered out quietly.

"What are you doing with those women?" he asked. "Do you realize their husbands are all chairmen of departments at the hospital?"

"Pearl brought them, I didn't know. They were paying me for lessons."

"They paid you, for what? Making a mess? Oh, Elaine, how could you do that to me? Don't ever embarrass me like that again."

He marched into the bedroom and slammed the door. Humiliated, I quickly made him a baloney and cheese sandwich, then grabbed the baby and ran down the two flights of stairs and drove to the unemployment office to collect my monthly $36.00 check. We went to the park and then wandered through the village. When we returned, the sandwich was gone and he had left for the hospital. Alone that night, shivering, wrapped up in an old green Army blanket, I huddled with my longed-for vodka, my sensitive stomach churning.

Stewart—thank God for Stew—pounded again on my kitchen window. "How's the decorating class going, beautiful?"

Trying to keep my composure, I told him Bob's reaction to the doctor's wives' art lessons.

"Well, it sounds like you've got yourself a bona fide lemon. You're going to have to learn to make the best goddamn lemonade known to man. By the way, good news, Computer Sciences is promoting me and we're going to look for a house to buy. I want to be your first decorating client."

"You'd trust me to do that?"

"You'll do great, better than us. My wife and I are not creative like you and could never do it by ourselves. She's all for it."

The neurosurgical rotation was demanding for Bob. The hours were brutal, and he said many of the patients were in a vegetative state after surgery. He became close to several residents in the full-time program and two weeks into it, came home unexpectedly, shaking. I rushed over and threw my arms around him.

"What happened today? Sit down. Honey, you're white as a sheet."

"John Flann, one of the neurosurgical residents, died today."

He told me that John had operated on a sixteen-year-old girl the previous night who expired. John was despondent and shot himself in the mouth that morning. The word around the hospital was that Ernest Hemingway had ended his life the same way.

John was the person Bob had become closest to in the program. He was a fifth-year resident, Bob's role model, ready to go out into the world and operate on spinal injuries and brain tumors.

"He had a family," Bob said. "A wife and three children. What'll they do now?"

Three days later we walked into the UCLA chapel for John's memorial, holding hands. Organ music and the aroma of lavender and gladiolas filled the church. Bob squeezed my hand as John's wife filed in, carrying her infant, papoose-style, with two toddlers by her side. Professors and residents followed. The pews were filled to capacity, everyone in a state of shock.

After John's death, Bob became obsessed with Hemingway, wanting to read his manuscripts and know more about why he killed himself. Sitting in a corner of the orange couch with the light of the floor lamp shining down, he devoured book after book, encircled by a ring of smoke, as if in a trance.

CHAPTER 4

Orders

Bob barely spoke for two weeks. The death of John Flann hung heavy. The baby was sleeping, and he and I sat together on the orange couch sipping coffee, with the stack of Hemingway books piled on the iridescent mosaic coffee table I had made. Bob hesitated, then stammering, blurted out. "I've been thinking: I might change my plans and not go into neurosurgery. Maybe OB-GYN; what do you think?"

I was silent, my eyes wide with surprise. This statement contradicted his life's goal. "That's quite a switch. I didn't know you liked the field that much."

He explained that in OB everyone's happy; the end result's almost always a healthy baby, not death or paralysis. And the training's only four years, not five. He said, "We could start our lives sooner and not be saddled with constant poverty, have more children."

I reached over and grabbed his hand. "I know how hard it's been for you, sweetheart."

The next day he went to the department of Obstetrics and Gynecology to discuss his decision to change his specialty. He was their number one boy, after all, and they were receptive. Within the month he received an admissions letter, accepting him into the four-year OB-GYN residency program at the Harbor General Hospital facility for UCLA.

Our ritual was to have Sunday dinner with my parents and two younger sisters, Deborah and Susan. Since we did not own a TV, we always stayed, and the whole family watched Alfred Hitchcock, then the news. The following Sunday at dinner, as Cindy gurgled and watched us from her playpen, we brought up the subject of our moving closer to the hospital. For the first few months, Bob drove 45 minutes on the 405 Freeway from our apartment in Westwood to Harbor General in Torrance. It was a depressingly long drive, passing industrial tracts and odiferous oil fields. We knew we should move, but Torrance seemed like a foreign land.

When we mentioned it to my father, he immediately got excited and told us it was a wonderful opportunity to buy property in that area. My father George had gone to law school in the thirties, but in Los Angeles during the land boom, instead of practicing law, he started a title company business. When I was a child, our dinner conversations revolved around the purchase of empty land and construction. The thirties and forties were an exciting time. Los Angeles was the new frontier, and my father had the foresight to create a business that dealt with the procurement of property.

"Prices are low in Torrance. By the end of four years, the value will have increased, giving you enough equity to buy anywhere."

"But we don't have money to buy a house."

"Your birthday's coming up, Elaine. I'll give you $2,000 as a gift." He told us that would be enough for a down payment and suggested we go the following week to search the area together.

Sporting his usual long Cuban cigar, my father George took us in his old maroon Chrysler down the 405, passing oil derricks in El Segundo and miles of empty, undeveloped land in Torrance. We met with a potbellied, bespectacled broker who drove us around in his beige Studebaker, showing us small homes in the new tracts of land. The following Sunday we met again, this time bringing the baby. We went first to a location next to Carson Boulevard. All the homes looked the same—without character. I told the broker we wanted to be close enough to the hospital that Bob could walk. I stayed in the car with the baby while Bob and the broker ran in and out of six or eight more houses. Finally, Bob pounded on the window with a big grin, motioning me to come out. "We've found a great one. You've got to see it."

I bundled up the baby and, carrying her, walked slowly from room to room. The tract was new and the houses similar to one another, but this particular one was at the end of the cul-de-sac, a little white cottage with a low fence skirting the grass by the sidewalk, and it had an apple tree in the backyard. Harbor General was four blocks away and the payments were less than if we had rented.

We took the plunge and bought it, reveling in our new little home. Bob was still earning very little, but more than his internship salary, and we could afford to eat. My days were busy painting rooms, unpacking boxes, and cooking for our little family. After dinner, we often walked through the neighborhood with Cindy in the stroller, and my lonely nights with vodka were but a memory.

After three months in the OB-GYN residency program, Bob seemed listless and bored, often coming home early. He appeared to be without purpose. "I feel ridiculous, but realize I've made a drastic mistake," he said. "OB's the same thing, day after day. I'm dying to go back and pursue the neurosurgical residency that I always dreamed about."

Just as this realization manifested itself, the Berlin crisis broke out and Bob received a registered letter from the U. S. Government, drafting him into the Army; the shock took days to digest.

Not knowing where to turn, we called William Longmire, the chief of surgery at UCLA, requesting a conference to discuss the situation. We sat together in the recesses of Doctor Longmire's grasscloth-wallpapered office, as Bob poured out his conundrum.

"The Air Force offers greater opportunities," Longmire said. "I'll call Oliver Niess, the Surgeon General, and an old friend from medical school. He'll help us."

Longmire picked up the phone in front of us, appraising General Niess of Bob's brilliance and surgical skills, and asked him to place Bob in a surgical position with the Air Force. Then he let us know that Niess would do his best.

We checked the mailbox every day and finally, after eight long months, the orders arrived. Bob was to report to the Air Force base in Laredo, Texas on the Mexican border, not as a surgeon, but as the only obstetrician/gynecologist on the base.

CHAPTER

5

Laredo

We had been squeezed inside the blue and white Ford for days, stopping at cheap motels, then at last the Texas state line and the long stretch of 109-degree heat. Our luggage was tied to the roof, the trunk stuffed, and the inadequate air cooler hung out the right front window. Wearing short pants and a T-shirt, Bob dripped with sweat as we barreled through the endless desert. I was six months pregnant with our second child, my belly protruding and hair slicked with perspiration, bare feet up on the dash while Cindy slept in the back seat. Bob hardly spoke. Uneasy, he was not sure of what lay ahead.

On the fourth day we saw the first sign that we were nearing Laredo, a Holiday Inn, with a photo of their pool on the billboard.

"We're here!" Bob shouted. "Let's stop. We can swim and stay the night."

He drove into the circular driveway, grabbed his suitcase, unstrapped Cindy and jumped out. I slowly emerged and, holding my two-year-old's hand, went to the desk and checked in. From our first-floor, floral carpeted room, Cindy and I could see Bob, already in the pool, waving and yelling, "The water's great, come on in."

The air-conditioned motel room was so seductive; we wallowed in our inexperienced version of luxury. I was secretly glad to have a safe place to hide. We stayed a month, until we found a place to live on the base and furniture arrived.

The house we found was small, of clapboard, near other service families, backing up to an open field of wild mesquite, with a clothesline decorating the weeds.

As we drove into the base of green prefab buildings, the guard saluted Bob who had come in as first lieutenant, with a silver bar on each shoulder. In a short time, he became a captain, with two bars. The only obstetrician on the air base, he was Doctor Popularity. The young married families were having babies, and the single men brought their girlfriends in droves to see Dr. Good.

Once settled, we scouted the area for our favorite foods. Bob and I had been avid pizza lovers, and in my pregnant state, cravings for the pies haunted me. We searched the yellow pages and found only one listing for pizza in the entire city. We got out the map, as though on a treasure hunt, drove to the outskirts of town, down a dusty road to an isolated industrial area, and found the Pizza Kitchen. It was the weekend, and ominously deserted.

Bob charged out of the car and pounded on their door. "Door's locked. Here's a number. We may have to be content with tacos for the next two years."

I thought, *How will we ever survive? We can't be the only ones in town who love pizza. What about the guys at the base?*

We had sold our little house in Torrance for a slight profit, and for the first time had money in the bank. Thinking of what my father would do, I said, "It might be a good investment."

"Elaine, you're crazy. We're in the Air Force and having another baby in three months."

"Let's call the owner," I said. "See how much he's asking." In

1962, women did not do the calling. It was up to the husband to be the aggressor.

"I don't want to do it, but if it means that much to you. . . . "

I felt life coming back; I needed to work, to be challenged. "Let's be brave, it'll be fun and we'll get a chef."

Reluctantly, Bob drove us back out to the Pizza Kitchen the following week and waiting for us in a rundown scarlet Oldsmobile was short, balding Mr. Benedetto, thrilled to meet a prospective buyer. He unlocked the high, carved double wood doors, and the sight of two giant tarantulas crawling up one wall immediately greeted us. The place obviously needed to be cleaned and painted, but the space was ample, and I saw possibilities. Bob looked at me, suggesting by his glance, *Do you really want to do this?*

After pointing out the negatives to Mr. Benedetto, he came way down on his price and practically paid us to take it off his hands. Bob said, "We'll think about it." But Benedetto took one look at me, and knew we were hooked.

As the man drove away, he flashed a wave out the window with a big smile on his happy round face. I sent him a deposit the following week and we suddenly found ourselves the proud owners of the Pizza Kitchen takeout parlor. . . . I had never made pizza in my life. We scratched our heads, looked at each other and said, "My God, what have we done?"

Cindy stayed in the playpen while we scrubbed the floors and cabinets. I went in alone with a roller and brush, painting the walls canary yellow and the cabinets bright orange. *Very Mexican*, I thought. By the weekend, when the paint had dried, Bob and I strapped on the dingy blue work aprons hanging in the closet of the ancient kitchen. We found sweet basil, oregano and other spices in the cupboard, and an antiquated, yellowed recipe to try. Little Cindy toddled around on the flour-strewn floor, chomping on our experimental pizza crust, while Bob and I stirred sauce in huge pots, much of it landing on my watermelon belly, and laughed hysterically. We discovered that sauce is smoother and tastes better cooked before putting it on the pies, then experimented with vegetables, cheeses, and sausage toppings. I made a four-foot high "OPEN" sign using the orange paint from the cabinets, and nailed it out front.

We advertised in the airbase newspaper for a pizza cook and within two days received a call from Tony Colonna, a short, dark-haired Sicilian chef from the officers' club, who grew up watching his mother make pizza. He needed the extra money to support his five children, and planned to come at 4:00 p.m. after work every day except Sunday.

Customers were scarce and we were desperate for business to pay for supplies and Tony's salary, so we put another ad in the Air Force paper. The Kitchen was too far from the base, and no one came. At this time, there had never been frozen pizza in markets before. Tony suggested we approach the commissary with the idea. They placed a small order. It sold out immediately, and they reordered. Customers told us that the 94 percent Mexican population in town would prefer their pizza to be spicier. We quickly realized the only way to adequately cater to their palate was to venture across the Rio Grande into Nuevo Laredo, Mexico. The guards stopped us at the border, inspected our car, licenses, and passports, and after that we were on our own to search for the vital ingredients. The streets were wide and traffic sparse, with roughly constructed stores along the sides of roads filled with potholes. It looked like a rundown, empty desert town, with all the signs in Spanish. We recognized the word *jalapeño* and parked the car directly in front of the shop. Inside we found huge vats of chilies in varying degrees of spiciness. The salesman was a sixteen-year-old Mexican boy. He greeted us enthusiastically, happy to practice his English and discuss our dilemma. We bought gallon cans of *jalapeños*, ranging from mild to the hottest green chili peppers, and included a case of cheap *DOS EQUIS cerveza* (Mexican beer). With our new spicy, south of the border toppings, we tried selling frozen to the markets in town. They ordered several pizzas, which sold out quickly, then reordered. We were at last in business.

Our baby was due the end of December, and we agreed that if I did not deliver by Christmas, Bob would induce labor. I was faced with the serious decision: should Bob deliver our child with only a single year of obstetrical training? There was only one obstetrician in town, whom we did not know; the rest of the population in Laredo went to midwives. I realized I had no alternative. I had to trust my husband.

So the day the Christmas ornaments came down, we packed a few things for Cindy and took her to stay with a neighbor who also had a two-year-old, then drove to the hospital as if going shopping for milk. A kind military nurse ushered me into a gray, windowless room with nothing but a plastic lounge chair and a two by two-foot steel table on wheels. Bob induced me and then disappeared. Fifteen minutes later he reappeared in his green scrub suit with an aide wheeling in a gurney. I climbed up, the nurse prepped me, and Bob came in again and stripped my membranes, saying, "There you go, Mrs. Good." He turned around to leave, and I grabbed his arm.

"Bob, I need you, please don't leave."

"Elaine, I'm working." He vanished again. I was left alone and rationalized that he had to objectify me. He was now the doctor, not the husband, but I was in a strange place and frightened. I needed both. The place was deserted, so cold and indifferent. I could not understand where everyone was.

I lay there thinking something would happen. He would come back, but after several hours, I got worried. Nothing was happening, and I wanted my husband. I needed him to hold my hand and tell me we were in this together and everything would be fine. I felt abandoned. I don't know how many hours passed until my contractions began. It seemed an eternity. I was alone. Finally, I called out: "Nurse!" And no one came. I lifted myself off the gurney, quietly wandered down the hall in my hospital gown, and found the nurse's aide.

"Where is everyone? Where's Dr. Good?"

"Doctor's checking other patients." She called the nurse who reappeared.

"How you doing, darlin'?" she asked.

"Please call Dr. Good. I need him." I went back to my cubicle; she followed and helped me onto the gurney.

My contractions started to get stronger and stronger. I was afraid to complain. After all, I was the doctor's wife, and thought he'd be angry if I caused a scene. I screamed soundlessly. The baby's head was pushing. Where was he?

"Please, call Dr. Good," I finally shouted. "The baby's coming." She ran out looking for him. He casually came in with a stethoscope around his neck and checked the baby's heart rate. "My God, you're ready," he said, "faster than I expected." And in a mad dash he rolled me, running down the long empty hall, directly into the delivery room and administered the local anesthetic himself. Within minutes, our son Glendon Robert was out, on my stomach, screaming. Bob bent down and we both cried. It was the 27th of December 1962.

Bob brought Cindy home from our neighbor's house the next day. I lay sleeping in the hospital at around 4:00 a.m. and woke up, startled, to the sound of my husband's footsteps strutting down the dimly lit linoleum hallway. *He must have had an emergency delivery.* I waited for him to come into my room to check on me, give me a kiss, or say something, anything. I called out, "Bob," but he passed so quickly. I lay there bereft, worried about my little girl home alone. He said a neighbor came over, but I always wondered . . .

A month after our baby Glen was born and anxious to meet other people, I made a little dinner party to meet the only other OB-GYN in town. He was a convivial, gray-haired, stocky Texan from Austin who came with his bubbly, petite Mexican wife. The conversation centered on hunting, the great pastime in the wilds of that Tex-Mex border town. The doctor bragged endlessly about his shooting prowess. The next morning he called to thank us for dinner and invited Bob to go hunting.

"But I don't own a gun, never even held one," Bob said.

"It's time you learn; the power will overwhelm you." He explained they would go out at sun-up on Sunday mornings and bring home enough dove and quail for a great feast. Bob was reluctant, but accepted the challenge. I worried about having a gun around the house, but did not want to squelch his enthusiasm or the camaraderie of his new friend.

He bought a twelve-gauge shotgun and went for instruction and target practice. In two weeks, at dawn on a foggy Sunday morning, the town doctor drove up in his gray Thunderbird. Bob hopped in with his shotgun and they drove to a hunting preserve on the outskirts of town. At the end of the day, they came back and dumped quail and dove in the sink from a sailcloth sack, Bob's face flushed with elation.

"We watched and waited," he said. "Then when the birds flew by in flocks, we shot like crazy, round after round. So much fun." He gutted and de-feathered each and I piled them into a deep pot, making a rich soup, adding bacon and onions with beer at the end.

On the third of their many outings, in preparation, Bob put his knapsack and twelve-gauge by the front door, and we went to bed early. He arose at 4:30 a.m. I heard him rustle around and dress quietly, then the front door closed, and I fell back to sleep. A subtle light awakened me, flashing under my closed bedroom door.

The miles of open field behind our airbase house crept into my mind. On that block, we were all open targets. Some neighbors kept guns poised by their windows in the event of a prowler. Shooting to protect one's life and property was said to be legal in that wild border town. I lay in silence as the light under my door persisted. I wondered if they had watched and waited. Did they know I was alone with the children? I heard a scratching movement . . . terror rushed through my body. I had to conjure my strength, plan my attack.

I arose from the bed with great force, flipped on the overhead light, picking up the heavy ceramic lamp from the nightstand with both hands, stretching my arms high above my head so the lamp could come down hard on the intruder. I kicked the door open with my strong right foot, and was shocked to discover my husband, meekly searching for his keys, using a flashlight so he would not wake me. Before I could stop it, the lamp came down and broke into a thousand pieces. Thank God it only brushed his shoulder and Bob was not injured or killed.

We had just eaten lunch on November 22, 1963, and a year had passed since our arrival. I was coaxing little Glen to take his first step while three-year old Cindy played nearby. The front door was open with sunshine streaming through, while the closed screen shielded us from the Texas insects. Our TV was turned on to a children's show. I glanced over as the program was interrupted with a news flash. John Kennedy had been shot in Dallas while driving, convertible top down in a motorcade.

Stunned by the news, I grabbed both children and locked the door. I had voted for Kennedy, was fond of him, and believed he was our hope for a new, safe America. The next day, there was a chill in the air. We were all grieving the loss of Kennedy. After their naps, seeking a distraction, I piled the children in the car and drove across town, down the isolated road, over the railroad tracks to the industrial area to check on our Pizza Kitchen. We arrived just after four. The streets were thronged with dark-skinned workers in colorful baseball caps, carrying lunch pails, coming out of the factories. From a distance, I noticed a mass of humanity swarming near the Pizza Kitchen. As I got closer, I realized that the throngs were a line, waiting to get in to our place, perhaps to get a snack or bring home dinner for their families. Tony had hired pretty Angelina to tend the counter while he was madly shoveling pizza into the brick oven. She was handing out *cerveza* to the guys in line. *Good move*, I thought. I could not believe my eyes. There was a whole world of life down there, and we were now an integral part of it. I parked the car and walked in carrying the baby, holding Cindy's hand.

"*Buenos dias*, Angelina."

"*Buenos dias*, Senora Bueno."

Tony looked up and gave me a big grin.

"I see business is booming," I said.

I gave Cindy a candy sucker from the bowl I had placed on the counter. I asked the men in line if there was something we could do to improve the pizza. Some suggested more *jalapeño*, others said spicy sausage, or more cheese. We lingered, and then I noticed the sun starting to set, and thought we'd better get home before dark. We piled back into the Ford and I sped away smiling, feeling a sense of accomplishment. The car sputtered and stopped a half mile away. I tried the ignition again and got it going, but the car was sluggish. I checked the gas, and the tank was half full. The car sputtered again, then stopped. I tried to start the motor, but it merely chugged.

Panic set in as I realized the front section of the car was sitting on the railroad tracks. I froze. The children were silent. *Do I take them out, run from the car and watch it get smashed by the train, causing a major train wreck?* There was no one in sight, only empty fields. We had no cell phone then. *Would Bob ever find us?*

In the distance I heard the faint rumble of a train approaching. I tried the car again, to no avail. The children must have sensed my fright, because both Cindy and the baby started crying. I tried the ignition again and again. . . . *Dear God, please help us!* I was just about to get out and grab the children, but decided to try one more time and somehow, finally, it started. I backed up instantly, just as the train rumbled by. We sat in a trance, watching. I let out a deep cry of relief. Then, from the back seat, I heard a faint, "Mommy, I'm so hungry."

We left Laredo in 1964. Tony, our chef, purchased the Pizza Kitchen, which continued to prosper by selling fresh to the factory locals and frozen to markets throughout the region.

The children and I flew back to Los Angeles without Bob. We landed amid a blazing sunset, clutching each other, as the freeways below flowed in circular patterns. Honeysuckle perfumed the air, and Los Angeles nights were still cool with temperate days. It was as though we had never been away.

Bob drove back through the hot desert alone. The second morning, from a pay phone in the lobby of his Motel 6, he called William Longmire at UCLA to quench the hammering in his unconscious to go back into neurosurgery, but Longmire was on sabbatical and would not be back for eight months. By the time Longmire arrived home, Bob had made the decision to continue with his residency in OB-GYN at the Harbor General Hospital facility for UCLA.

CHAPTER

6

The Hidden Gun

Bob and I let the waves wash over our feet on the wind-swept beach at Ensenada, Mexico, early on a September morning. We shared our love of the sea and stole a few days to savor the blue Pacific before he began his second year of obstetrical residency. Our third child, Bradley, had been born six weeks prior, and Bob's mother, Elsie, lived so close that we grabbed the chance to escape for a weekend.

We strolled in the early morning deserted beach, filling our pockets with shells, and spotted a fisherman casting his line by the water's edge. As we approached him, we saw a small, dark-skinned woman in an orange striped serape crouched down on the sand, next to a stove constructed from a sheet of steel, over an open fire. The fisherman gently dislodged his catch, cleaned it with seawater, and threw small chunks onto her make shift stove. I salivated as I watched her wrap the fish in a corn tortilla.

"It looks too good to pass up," I said, remembering the fresh Mexican food we had grown to love in Laredo.

"Wouldn't touch it if I were you," Bob said. "I'm sticking to my banana."

"You're missing a great treat," I said, as I gobbled it down.

Six weeks later, fatigued beyond the usual new-mother syndrome, Bob noticed the whites of my eyes had turned yellow, and took me to have a liver function test. I had contracted what they called in 1964 "infectious hepatitis."

"I knew that fish was bad news," Bob said. "You were crazy to eat it, no sanitary facilities." He took me home, then ran back to Harbor Hospital to continue with his day, leaving me sick and alone with my three children under four. That night he gave himself and the children gamma globulin injections, hoping it would protect them from catching my hepatitis.

Debilitated, I lay around in my nightgown and robe, day after day. The first three months were hell. When the baby cried, I could hardly get up, sometimes crawling to his room to feed him. Often, I kept him with me all night to make it easier. Nurses were expensive, and babysitters refused to come. Even my mother was afraid of catching my hepatitis.

Bob was glad when his second rotation sent him to City of Hope Hospital in Duarte for cancer research, an hour away. For several months he stayed all week, returning home on Fridays in his starched white coat with his stethoscope hanging out of the lower pocket. I would dress for the first time all week, do my hair and put on makeup and perfume. As he drove up, I'd call out, "Daddy's home" and we all ran to the door, kissing and hugging. But by Monday he could hardly wait to climb into the Ford, light up a Pall Mall and drive away as we watched and waved.

Bob returned to Harbor General for his next rotation. I was healing but still at home, a stranger to the outside world. My spirit had faded into quiet depression, and my body blew up, misshapen from a year of no exercise and excessive eating to heal my liver.

Bob's hours became longer each day, until one night I called the hospital at 2:00 a.m., holding my breath as the nurse answered.

"Obstetrical unit. Sorry dear, Dr. Good checked out hours ago."

Unable to sleep, my damaged liver prevented me from even thinking of drinking my old vodka to knock me out. I sat in my crimson robe enveloped in darkness, holding my infant, smelling of baby powder, and waiting. Finally, at 4:30 a.m., I heard the car drive up and the door gently close.

He snuck in quietly; tie loosely hanging, the stench of scotch and tobacco on his breath, shirttails out and his starched white lab coat crumpled. Carefully removing his shoes, he tiptoed through the small living room, spotting me on the sofa in the silent shadows. "Hi, what are you doing up?"

I was mute.

"I said, what are you doing up?"

Finally, I heard myself answer in a frightened, tiny, high voice. "Were you in an accident? Where have you been?"

His eyes avoided mine. "At the hospital, delivering an elderly primigravida with preeclampsia. Why don't you go to bed?"

I sat there, catatonic. Bob pulled off his tie in a huff. He told me that he was on his way to the car when an aide came running after him to see a patient in emergency. He ran back thinking it would only take a few minutes, but she was preeclamptic and in shock. He stayed with her until she delivered.

"What else could I do? Come on, let's get to bed," he said.

I wanted to believe him. Grabbing his hand, I pulled him toward the bedroom. "Glad you're home, honey."

Two nights later, there was another excuse, and the scenario repeated itself. I drew deeper into my shell. Usually, he came home after the children were in bed, and I served him dinner, seldom speaking, as he smoked and told me about his day. He could not look me in the eye. I felt like a non-person. A solemn silence became my refuge.

It took more than a year for my liver function tests to be normal, but exhaustion continued to haunt me. We still needed the income, so I hired babysitters and returned to my decorating business. The days were long with the resource showrooms over an hour away from our new house. I looked for trees to park under to take my midday nap.

I finished decorating Stewart's home, did a school, and designed several offices of medical friends going into practice. But the materialism of always shopping and searching for fabrics and furniture began to grate on me. I yearned for the day when money was no longer an issue and I could pursue my painting.

Realizing I would need to be my own support system, I started dieting, working out, and signed up for a painting class one night a week with UCLA Extension. Cindy was now five, Glen three, and the baby, Bradley, the image of his father, almost two.

Bob came home one night unexpectedly while I was getting ready to go to my class. I was glad he was home, but it did not dawn on me that he had never been alone with the children. When I returned, he had a cigarette hanging out of his mouth as he held the screaming, malodorous baby while the other two ran screaming around the house.

"When I'm home, I want you here," he shouted. "You know I can't deal with the kids." I realize now that men of that era rarely were involved in childcare.

The following week, I had a sitter. Bob came home around 9:00 p.m., just as I was returning from class. I greeted him with a hug and told him I had brought something to show him. I placed my very first finished painting on the kitchen counter. With the smell of fresh oil paint permeating the room, I turned out all the lights except the bright ones shining on the canvas. I served him the chocolate chip cookies I had baked that afternoon and poured each of us a cup of mint tea.

"Come sit with me," I said, as I pulled up his chair. "I want to show you what I've been doing." I was proud of the small canvas, a subtle butterfly in shades of yellow and pink.

Still in his tie and lab coat, he sat pondering the painting for several minutes. Without looking at me, he munched on his cookie, lit a cigarette, took a long slow drag and boldly said, "You should stay home where you belong. The painting is terrible, get rid of it."

It was like he had stabbed me in my gut. I tried to swallow his comment, unable to speak. When I mentioned his response to Charles Garabedian, my esteemed instructor, he came back with a comment I will always remember. "The painting is great. Better to get rid of the husband than the painting."

That work of art ended up in Stewart's new home as my housewarming gift. It was the early 1960s, and my goal was to make the marriage work. At that time, I believed to be divorced was an admission of failure. In my milieu, a woman alone was frowned upon and powerless. I also felt that the children needed their father, and they were always my primary concern.

Bob finished his residency and accepted a position as a fulltime assistant professor at UCLA hospital, but after several months, he left to join Jesse Garber, a prominent gynecologist in Beverly Hills.

At last, after thirteen years of training and two years of military service, he started to earn a living. We relocated to a modest Dutch Colonial home on a quiet, tree-lined cul-de-sac in Brentwood, a suburb of Los Angeles. He came home most evenings. The children and I still ran to the door, excited to see him, although his response was not what I hoped.

Marching in, the new practicing doctor, wearing his Brooks Brothers suit, white shirt and pinstriped tie, would greet us with a broad grin.

"Hi guys! How's everyone tonight?"

All four of us would run to the door with open arms as the kids responded in unison, "We're great, Daddy," jumping up and down. "Read us a story."

Totally ignoring them, Bob would say, "Elaine, I've got to have a drink and be alone, it's been a long day. 40 patients after two surgeries, and I have a patient in labor."

He was happy to be home but drained physically and emotionally. Other doctors were sending their wives to him, and I realized he was overwhelmed by his immediate success. I was proud to be his wife, and knew he felt a great responsibility to his patients. I tried to do everything to make him comfortable.

"I'll give the kids a bath while you relax. Dinner's in the oven."

"Get me a scotch first, okay?"

"Daddy's had a long day; he's tired and needs to rest. Come on, the bubbles are waiting." We all thirsted to spend time with him, but he craved silence with his Macnish and cigarettes.

Bob had grown up in a simple, working class environment and found many of the affluent patients in his Beverly Hills practice to be high-strung and demanding. I often sensed that he longed for the simplicity of his hometown of Long Beach, California. As the months progressed, he became more and more silent, frequently disappearing, obsessed with going fishing, the one activity he had shared with his aged father. As a family we often joined him, and those were good times, but I became frightened as his tension mounted. He was on edge all the time. I rarely saw him without a smoldering Pall Mall in his hand.

Sharing our king-size bed with Bob was like sharing the bed of a tense stranger smelling of tobacco who once in a while made his way over to my side. Sometimes I was the aggressor, trying to stay connected, at least sexually; but usually his aloof coldness repelled me, and we lay so far from one another that, at arm's length, I could hardly reach him. We shared the children and our friends, but we were not soulmates, only partners leading parallel lives.

While unpacking boxes after moving into our new home, I discovered a large oblong case labeled: "fishing tackle." Inside, I had finally found the gun from his hunting expeditions in Laredo. A violent scene flashed before me, and an immediate instinct told me to get rid of it. I carefully picked up the gun, carrying it in my arms like a baby, out to our garage next to the house. I climbed the unfinished wooden staircase to a musty attic with high beams smelling of old unpainted wood. I thought, *What a perfect place for an art studio,* envisioning sneaking up to paint when the children were in school.

Under the single dormer in that raw attic, I discovered an inset window seat covered with a faded red and green plaid cushion. Opening the lid, I uncovered a storage compartment large enough to carefully place the twelve-gauge shotgun. I covered it with magazines, then lowered the lid and replaced the dusty cushion.

CHAPTER

7

My Lemonade

The night was blustery and my four, six and eight-year-old children were sleeping. Earlier, I'd told them I would be in the attic above the garage if they needed me. During the afternoon, I had stretched and primed a large canvas and made sketches as they played in the yard. Alone at last in my newfound workspace, I checked, and Bob's gun was still hidden in the window seat. I sat in the old green wicker chair left by the former owner and marveled at the high beams, the canvas about to be attacked, and the quiet.

On a piece of glass I'd taped around the edges, I squirted out several colors from new tubes of oil paint, then poured turpentine and linseed oil into aluminum containers. Picking up my largest brush, I dabbed into the burnt umber, smearing it with titanium white and slapped it on the canvas in massive, broad strokes.

Just then, I heard Bob's car drive up the cul-de-sac and turn into the garage. The door slammed, and then all was quiet. In several minutes, heavy footsteps marched up the creaky stairwell. He must have noticed the light on upstairs.

"What's going on up here?" Bob yelled.

"Hi, thought I'd surprise you with my new studio." Exhilarated, I said, "Like it?" I rushed over and gave him a hug.

"What are you doing up here in this filthy attic? Come in the house where you belong and get my dinner."

Shaken, I followed him into the house with my head down, placing his dinner on the table, and then silently sat and watched him eat.

I was too embarrassed to confide in my friends about the state of our marriage. They were all married. On the outside, I tried to make everything look perfect and create the myth of the happy home. I was afraid to confront him, fearing he would leave. I felt the children were my gift, each special in their own way. Little dark-haired Cindy was quite a dancer, and adorable in her pink tutu. And Glen, old beyond his six years, so smart, he seemed to know everything and, as he grew, would become a baseball and tennis player. My youngest, Bradley, also athletic, liked to juggle and played the guitar. Those three were my life.

We started skiing as a family, but Bob could not seem to catch on. For Christmas holidays he went, but on weekends he found excuses, so I took the children alone. The nights before those trips, we piled our skis on the roof rack of the car. I made fresh popcorn and picked them up at lunchtime from school on Fridays. We drove the seven hours up to Mammoth Mountain, singing with John Denver and Jim Croce on the tape deck while munching the popcorn. The next morning, we headed for the lifts and skied a few runs together. After lunch we scattered, exploring the mountain on our own, until the end of the day when we met down at the lodge. Back at the hotel, we changed into bathing suits and plunged into a hot jacuzzi, then dressed and went for dinner at one of the raucous dives in town. Those were my favorite times.

Bob's new medical partner, Jesse, had a lavish two-story stone house with a pool in Westwood Village. Impressed by its grandeur, and feeling powerful now that he was finally in practice, Bob longed to show the world he had made it, and wanted what

Jesse had. I loved our little Dutch Colonial, but he pushed me to look for a larger home. He also might have realized how despondent I had become and wanted to engage me in a new project.

The heavyset, 50-something, blonde real estate broker picked me up in her rundown, brown Cadillac, and drove me from one house to another in our price range. None were at all what Bob had in mind. She finally said, "Mrs. Good, this search is futile; the big house you're looking for with a pool will cost far more than you can afford."

That night at dinner I told Bob about the futility of our search and said, "Why don't you take the money we've saved and build that fishing boat you've always wanted?"

"I'd love that! I've been dreaming about a 24-foot sport fisher with a flying bridge and marlin tower for years."

Bob immediately found a boat builder, relishing the challenge, and when it was completed, we christened it with friends and cheap champagne. All five of us walked the plank to the shiny new blue sport fisher, carrying our fishing poles and backpacks. Bob had brought small fish as bait and patiently helped us thread our hooks, then showed us how to cast lines off the side of the boat. We caught a variety of small fish and cooked them on the two-burner boat stove. The open seas mesmerized me as we trolled slowly, while the diesel engine was running. In the evening, we sat on the deck together as the children slept in their bunks. We marveled at the beauty of the moon shining on the open sea and the reflection of dim lights from other boats, sharing our thoughts about the magnificence of the day. When the engine was finally off, the boat rocked with the churning sea, and the only sound in the darkness was the water lapping against the boat's hull. Then, startling our reverie, each of my two boys came up on deck, one after the other: "Mommy, my tummy hurts." I was feeling a little off-kilter myself, but did not want to mention it, and ruin our idyllic evening. Suddenly all three of us in unison started heaving uncontrollably. With both hands slapping his brow, Bob shouted, "Goddammit, if you're gonna vomit, get over to the stern. Stop messing up my new boat; puke off the rail."

The following year, 1972, on a fall day, while driving through Pacific Palisades, after delivering eight-year-old Bradley to his guitar lesson, I discovered a street on the bluff which ran parallel to the ocean overlooking the sea, called Corona Del Mar. I had always had a love affair with the ocean, and on that short street I found a large, wild plot of empty land with giant eucalyptus trees. I got out and tromped through high weeds toward the cliff's edge. The smell of the sea and salt air, along with the expansiveness of the horizon engulfed me. I went back the next day with a book and blanket, propping myself up against a tree trunk where I stayed for hours. It became my sacred place. Sometimes I napped; other times I lugged canvas and paints, trying to reproduce the splendor of the site.

After several months, on our way to the beach one Sunday, I brought the family. Tumbling out of the car, the children gravitated toward the edge of the high cliff, all three running from tree to tree. Bradley brought his net and found butterflies to chase.

"Hey, Mom, look, we can see Catalina Island," Glen said, pointing out to sea.

I sat on the weeds under my favorite tree watching, just waiting for Bob's response.

"I feel like we're in the ocean; what a great find," he said. "Wonder who owns it?"

I drove my parents out the following week, warning mother to wear her tennis shoes. Looking over the edge of the cliff, Mother remarked, "It's so high; think the children will be safe?"

"We'll build a fence," I said. Then turning to my father, "Think you could find out who owns it?"

He promptly researched it through the Department of Records, and found the owner, letting us know that the area was on the San Andreas fault line and the street had been the site of several serious landslides. Nevertheless, we took a chance and made an offer. For Christmas of 1972, we were the proud owners of that parcel of land. I remembered Stewart's instruction to me fifteen years before: *If I had a lemon, I'd better make the best goddamn lemonade known to man.* That land was going to be my lemonade. It teetered on the edge while our marriage was teetering.

To design and build a house on our cliff was daunting, but I sensed that I must have been an architect in my former life because designing that residence felt so natural. I had decorated homes and offices, but never designed or built a complete house from scratch. I chose a contractor whose preference was working directly with homeowners.

We spread the floor plans out on the dining room table, and for months worked out every detail. Long after everyone was in bed at night, I would sneak down to the plans and move bedrooms and add closets, wondering what else we might have forgotten. My contractor took on only one job at a time and did not mind helping with permits.

When construction commenced, I took the children to school each day and went directly to the job site to find our builder, with a full crew pounding away. The scent of fresh lumber became my aphrodisiac. They worked so fast, I prayed for rain so that we would have a day to catch our breath, but in L.A. it rarely rains. In five months, the construction project, including pool and landscaping, was complete. I made the stained glass window over the high, mahogany double front doors myself, and did the landscaping design, filling the front courtyard with jacaranda trees to bloom in spring and crimson bougainvillea to climb the walls. I put a red rose garden on the left and vermillion azaleas against the house. In the rear, by the cliff's edge, I planted honeysuckle to perfume the nights as we watched the pounding surf by moonlight. I wanted every detail to be a work of art.

In spite of all my misgivings, it was my greatest desire that life would be better, and we would start anew in this splendid place. When at last we slept in our new home with views of the open sea and smells of the salt air, the only sounds we heard were the Pacific's waves crashing below.

It was 1972, and it had taken us fifteen years to get to that point. We were lounging in the sun by our Mexican tiled pool one day, in shorts and straw hats, watching the children swim.

"Now that the house is finished, we're settled, and you're finally earning a living," I said, "I've decided to give up my decorating business and just be the painter I've always dreamed about."

Bob rubbed his eyes, pulled a Pall Mall from his pocket, lit it, and looking out at the azure sea, said, "That's absurd, why would you ever want to do a stupid thing like that? Painting is what children do in kindergarten. Better to stick with your decorating, and you're earning good money."

A sharp pain jabbed through the left quadrant of my abdomen. I could not combat him, or I knew he would walk out. Silence was my only response.

I had a good friend, Merle Miller, who painted, and after a time I quietly joined her small group of talented women artists in Venice. After three years, I rented my own studio on the corner of Millwood and Abbott Kinney, also in Venice. It was a storefront, twelve by thirty feet, with twelve-foot ceilings and storage racks in the back corner. My large wooden easel, holding a major painting, sat in the center of the splattered cement floor. Next to it was a rolling kitchen cart laden with a basket of oil paints, bottles of turpentine, copal medium, linseed and stand oils, plus two large soup cans filled with brushes of all sizes. Another easel sat off to the side for small works. The windows facing the street were horizontal, and up high on the wall. I had a wrought iron gate installed in front of the door so I could be safe when leaving it ajar for air. My corner with its high crime rate was, at that time, considered to be the "war zone" of Venice. By the entrance, I had a narrow daybed covered in a madras stripe for a couch, and a small steel desk from my father's office.

I wore one of Bob's old white lab coats from his med school days, which became encrusted with paint, and invited him to come to the studio, but he always said he was too busy. He never understood what I could possibly be doing there. So I reached out to friends, one after the other, to sit for portraits. They loved it, felt important, even lionized, and I played my classical tapes at last, with no one to tell me to shut them off.

Around this time in 1973, there were rumblings of the women's movement. No one among my married friends discussed it. They were too frightened they might lose their husbands. But my new artist friends were talking about it. I realized I had been the quintessential caregiver after studying Gail Sheehy's *Passages.* She talked about this period of awakening, giving us permission to question our futures as we never had before. Betty Friedan in 1963 had written about the empty life syndrome in her book *The Feminine Mystique:*

> *"Each suburban wife struggled with it alone. As she made the beds, shopped for groceries, matched slipcover material, ate peanut butter sandwiches with her children, chauf-*

> *feured Cub Scouts and Brownies, lay beside her husband at night—she was afraid to ask even of herself the silent question—"Is this all?"*

It seemed like she was talking about me. Then, after seeing *The Stepford Wives* movie, I realized that I was trying to hold on to Bob by quietly being the quintessential "Stepford Wife," a robot-replica of myself: perfect, beautiful, cleaning constantly, and silent.

I had played the piano as a child, and at last we had room for a baby grand in our new living room. I saved money from my design jobs for two years and finally bought a used Steinway and started playing again. It was our musical period, and Bob discovered the guitar. The last time we both played at the same time, he stomped out saying; "I can't hear my own guitar with your pounding on that miserable piano."

Our neighbors invited us to share their box at the Hollywood Bowl. Usually I gave my regrets, knowing Bob disliked the symphony and would not allow me out at night without him. However, on one occasion, after reading my women's movement books, I told him I was going, and he reluctantly agreed to come.

As the throngs milled around, we spread our dinner out on the small table provided by the Bowl, lit a candle, and ate our fried chicken and potato salad. When dinner was finished, we folded the table to the side and snuffed the candle out. The lights dimmed, and all was quiet except for the sounds of crickets in the distant bushes. As the Tchaikovsky concert commenced, I gazed up at the night sky teeming with stars, feeling blessed to be in the company of other classical devotees, and was overwhelmed by the passion of the instrumental sounds.

Unaware of my silent sobs, Bob put his hand on my shoulder. He whispered, "What's wrong, why are you shaking?" I put my finger up to my lips. "What's going on with you?" he demanded.

Wrapped up in emotion, I realized all that I had given up: my precious music, my art, and my very being. When the music stopped, I grabbed his hand, put my mouth to his ear, covering it with my other hand, and in the half-darkness whispered, "I've missed my music, and I've missed *me*."

I did not know how or when, but I just knew I could not spend the rest of my life sublimated. Ironic that it was at the Hollywood Bowl, where my mother told me she had gone into labor the night I was born, and the very place Bob proposed, at the Spring Sing of 1956.

CHAPTER

8

Leaping into Space

On the outside we were the golden couple, on everyone's invitation list. Mike, a psychiatrist, and Sue, an interior designer who lived up the street, invited us to a small dinner at their home. Floor-length dresses were the fashion that year, and it was nearing Christmas so, feeling glamorous, I wore my new scarlet velvet ankle-length.

In their blue dining room with white wainscoting, Sue had set the table all in white, except for blue plates to match the walls. After drinks, a cheese platter, and crisp bacon wrapped around chicken livers, she sat me next to Zachary, a short, olive-skinned professor from the college. Bob sat next to his petite, vocal wife. When I told Zachary I was a visual artist, his eyes lit up.

"Hey, I'm a painter. What do you work in?"

"I paint in oils. Studio's in Venice."

"Would you let me see your work? Friday's my day off. We could have lunch. Your studio's in the heart of some great restaurants."

At first, I said no, thinking Bob would not approve. But I was curious, and the thought of someone coming to see my work excited me. When Friday arrived, I was frantically trying to finish a new painting at noon when Zachary tapped on my iron gate. His voice was low and brisk as he peered through the bars.

He was casual, wore a gray T-shirt and jeans. He smelled of after-shave and mint gum.

"Hi, are you in there?" he said, peering through the bars. "Can we eat before I come in? I'm starved. Didn't get breakfast."

"Sure," I said as I nervously greeted him, and locked the gate, leaving the solid door ajar to allow the turpentine fumes to dissipate. The boulevard was full of artists' studios, galleries and restaurants, teeming with activity. We dashed over to Hal's on the next block. It was the hip new eating place, with polished black cement floors, high ceilings, and hanging on the walls were huge paintings by local artists. Zachary insisted I call him Zack, and we jabbered about our mutual love of art.

"I'm a non-objective abstractionist, paint in acrylic, similar to Rothko, only smaller," Zack said. "What about your work?"

"Gosh, I never thought of categorizing it. I guess I'm a figurative expressionist, in oils." He told me he was a transplanted New Yorker and had grown up sneaking into museums to ogle the art as a kid. To him, being an artist was a special pursuit. He was excited to tell me about the galleries, and what was going on in New York.

"You've got to get there; it'll change your life, Elaine. I'm telling you, it's the center of the art world."

My sphere had become so narrow with Bob, the children, and our few married friends' superficial dinner party conversations that I savored every moment with Zack. He was full of enthusiasm, open and casual. He listened to what I was saying, appeared interested, and his eyes reflected warmth and concern.

We came back to the studio, and he spent an hour inspecting my paintings as I watched him pensively examine each canvas.

"I'm not used to figurative work," he said. "I feel it's better to paint what you feel than what you see."

He seemed anxious, then suddenly blurted out, "Gotta get

going," and was gone in a flash. Mystified, I looked at my watch and realized it was almost time for the boys to get home from school and I wanted to be there.

The next morning, I was making peanut butter and jelly sandwiches and scrambling eggs. It was just before eight when Zack called.

"It was great to see your work yesterday; you inspired me. I ran home and painted till midnight." He told me that he wanted to show me what he was doing and asked if I could come to his house on Friday.

The following week, I found his gray Spanish-style home nestled among lush trees. The kitchen table was covered with newspapers, and a 16″ x 24″ small canvas with diffuse colors blended in a striated pattern was boldly propped up. He wanted my reaction, and said, "No one's ever honest about another's art."

I told him I felt it lacked depth. His surface was flat and screamed for more layers of pigment to create vitality and luminosity.

"It's great to be able to discuss my work with you," he said. We went to lunch at the Country Mart, and he called the next morning again.

"I've been thinking, how would you feel about my renting space in your studio to paint Friday afternoons? I'm too inhibited in my kitchen. My wife's afraid I'll drip on the floor."

I was surprised at this and immediately responded with an emphatic "no." "I like painting alone." Thinking of ways to dissuade him, I said, "You might not like my music. I am a classical addict, especially opera."

"So am I." There was a long silence.

"Well, I certainly couldn't charge you."

"How about if I buy lunch? That wouldn't quite pay the rent, but it would be something."

That excited me. Bob and I rarely went out and eating in restaurants sounded like fun.

"I might consider it if you'd allow me to paint your portrait."

"Hey, I'd love that. Never been painted."

I waited a week and weighed the pros and cons, feeling that every minute in the studio was precious, and knew that with Zack there, I would not get as much painting done. Bob was away most of the time, and silent when he was home. I thirsted for conversation but, still, I worried how Bob would react to my having Zack for a studio mate. But then I rationalized: *nurses, secretaries and women patients surround Bob every day. Only one afternoon a week is no big deal. How bad could that be*?

When Zack called, I told him we were on for Fridays. "I'll bring my supplies," he said. "What are your favorite operas? I'm loaded with tapes."

The first month, we worked in the studio diligently. At our lunches, we discussed what and who was exhibiting in New York. There were occasionally remnants of the New York art scene showing up in Los Angeles. One day, we dashed over to La Brea to see the first SAMO exhibition by graffiti artist Jean-Michel Basquiat and grabbed a hot dog on the way. We came back to the studio and I immediately squeezed out fresh pigment onto my palette, and while Zack set up his canvas on the side easel, I slipped in a Mozart tape.

I returned home those Friday evenings crammed with information about a different way of life. I was alive and more open, almost dancing as I prepared dinner, holding my head a little higher and humming tunes from *Carmen* and *La Bohème*. Bob and the children noticed my glow. Seated around the kitchen table, seventeen-year-old Cindy said, "Mom, you're so happy lately, what's going on?" I blushed, trying to sound unfazed.

"I have a new friend sharing my studio on Friday afternoons. He's smart, from New York, and I'm learning so much about the art world."

Bob looked up from his spaghetti, not uttering a word, and lit a cigarette. Inhaling, he tilted his head back, and blew smoke straight up toward the ceiling.

Zack suggested I jot my thoughts down to unlock my pent-up emotions. Said it would free me to be more creative. I bought a brown leather journal and spent a few minutes each morning in the studio writing before I went to work, then slipped it into the top drawer of my steel desk.

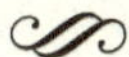

The following year, 1978, we were a busy family, getting ready for our oldest child to start college. Cindy decided on Sarah Lawrence College in Bronxville, one half-hour from New York City. I went with her to help her get settled in the dorm, then took the train into Manhattan and stayed at the Wyndham in Midtown.

At that time, the galleries were mainly in SoHo. The September wind was wild and howling my first day alone in the city as I went downtown by cab. Following Zack's instructions, apprehensively, I arrived at West Broadway, the center of the gallery area, and saw mobs congregating outside the 420 Building. Jumping out, I followed the crowd into Leo Castelli's gallery on the second floor, scrutinizing Roy Lichtenstein's large paintings of room settings. The women collectors were obvious in their long furs and high heels, hanging onto the arms of men in black overcoats. Most of the artists wore simple black leather and boots. I followed the mobs from floor to floor. One of Andy Warhol's early silent films was being shown on the third floor, and John Alexander's figurative landscapes were on the fourth. I walked across the street, down the block to Nancy Hoffman's gallery. She had a floor installation that encompassed the whole gallery. I slipped a gallery guide into my purse to go over later.

The next day, following the guide, I walked down Fifth Avenue, peering into the fancy shop windows. Turning onto 57th Street, I found the galleries. George Segal's painted plaster figures were showing at Sidney Janis Gallery, Chuck Close's huge, early dot portraits were at Pace, and Al Held's geometrical abstractions were at the Andre Emmerich Gallery. I was on a great high, so excited I could hardly breathe.

The clerk at my hotel explained the subway and gave me a map. The next day, I found the Fifth Avenue entrance and bravely marched down the steps to the N and R subway trains. Returning to SoHo, I followed the guide and explored the galleries on Broome, Spring, and Prince Streets. I felt like a gluttonous child, having discovered ice cream for the first time.

I returned home to the isolation of my Venice studio and immediately ordered several 48″ x 60″ stretched canvases, inspired to find my own voice. When Friday afternoon came, I exploded with tales of my adventures to Zack. He was proud of my bravery. It was as though he had held my hand at every step in the Big Apple.

During that winter, I took Bradley skiing as a treat for his thirteenth birthday. We flew to Portland, then took the train up to Vancouver and stayed at an old restored castle, the Banff Springs Hotel. It was good to be alone with one child, without the demands of household duties. On the third night, Brad and I had eaten dinner in the hotel dining room and were relaxing in the room after a full day racing through fresh powder on the hill. The phone rang by the bed in the room. It was Bob in a low, angry voice.

"Having a good time?"

"Hi. Everything alright? What's up?"

"I went into your studio today."

"You what? How'd you get in? I invited you and you always refused. You broke in?"

I imagined him walking among my things, curiously inspecting the paintings. He must have found the portraits of all my friends, and the obvious one of Zack. And then I realized he most likely had opened my desk and found my journal.

"I know about you and Zack," he said.

I felt sick at his accusation, after all those years of trying so hard to be the perfect wife. Before Brad could see my stricken horror, I grabbed my ski jacket and ran down the back stairwell of the hotel and sat outside on a stoop in the icy cold. I was incensed that Bob would invade my private space. I had no reason to feel guilty but knew that writing about sharing the love of art with Zack, and my elation at having him in the studio on Fridays would hurt Bob. I wondered if, when he read my fantasies, he found them thrilling or horrifying.

Incensed by his invasion, my response to Bob was indignation. Always secretly afraid of him, and after 21 years of suppression, an unexpected, calm resolve came over me. Zack had given me so much confidence that I now had a deep strength and righteousness.

Several days after our return, I sat at the walnut desk in our small study in the semi-darkness of the midnight hour as the children slept and waited for Bob to get home. I surrounded myself with my women's movement books as I rehearsed my speech. It was late, as usual. He came in, immaculately dressed in his good gray suit, white shirt and fancy tie. I had learned long ago never to ask where he had been, or he would march back out.

"What are you doing up at this hour?" he asked.

Very calmly, I heard myself recite the simple but life-changing words I had rehearsed. "Sit down, Bob, please. It's been a long time coming, but I know now that I need to be on my own. I want you to leave. I want a divorce."

His eyes widened in surprise. I watched him crumple into the spindle chair next to the desk, his arms flopping into his lap. Fearing his silences and quick temper, I had always shied away from confrontation.

"Why would you ever want me to leave? I thought we were happy," he said. "And what about our new home. . . . It's Zack, you're in love with him, I know it."

"I don't know. He has just allowed me to be myself and helped me to realize how locked up and empty I've been." Sensing the tension, Jake, our golden retriever, started barking. I had never seen Bob so shaken. His face was ashen. He looked at me as though he was seeing me for the first time.

"Please, Elaine, let's give it another try." No one had ever rejected this man. "You'll be sorry. You'll never find anyone as smart as me."

"I don't care," I said. "I'm just so sick of being alone, of being left out of life." I could hear my voice rising. "I'm starving for someone to share my feelings with, to love, and feel the warmth of sweet, caring sex."

"We'll go into couples therapy and work on the marriage. I'll even take dancing lessons. You always wanted us to dance together."

I slowly calmed down, gaining control. "You've negated everything I stand for and have not been supportive, in spite of my working all those years so you could be a doctor."

I did not mention his affairs; I just could not go there. His pleas were surprising. I realized that after all those years I had tried to make the marriage work, he was now making the effort. I could not turn my back on that.

"Okay, we'll give it a few months," I said.

I asked Zack not to come during that time, while I sorted things out. Bob actually went to the County Museum with me, along with the children, on Mother's Day, without complaining. I knew that he had no background in the arts. The creative process was a mystery to him. How could he understand what I was about? But after all those years of trying to please him and hold our family together, I was worn out. It was too late.

We made one last venture to recover the sweetness and rented a bareboat, out of Tortola in the Virgin Islands. During the day, we all snorkeled in the sunlight and explored the island. At night, we danced at Stanley's to the steel band and ate lobster. I could not help being pensive and silent. When everyone went to bed, I huddled in my bunk and continued with my reading; this time, Marilyn French's *The Women's Room*. By the end of the trip, it was clear that I needed to follow through with my plan to pursue my own dreams. Cynthia went back to school, and as winter approached, we were alone with Glen and Brad.

"I've decided to take the boys skiing Christmas vacation so that we don't upset them more than necessary," I said. "While we're gone, please go through the house and gather your things. Take anything you want. When we get back, I would like you to be totally moved out."

He realized that the fight was over, no storming out this time. He stared at me in disbelief and in his quiet, controlled manner, reluctantly agreed.

Sixteen-year-old Glen and I took our skis off and got into the gondola, which lifted us up to the highest point of Mammoth Mountain, the most challenging Black Diamond run, a sheer cliff called the Cornice. As we rode up, panic gripped me. Exiting the gondola, we skied a short way to meet the lip. Peering down at the silent, white world below, Glen brazenly jumped the eight-foot Cornice, flying down the mountain, as I stood there transfixed with fear.

Standing on the ledge, searching the birds and cobalt sky, I saw that Glen had stopped mid-way down, and was motioning to me with one arm.

"Come on, Mom, you can do it."

As I contemplated my leap into space, I asked myself, *can I jump that eight-foot lip?* I had to, I was committed, and there was no turning back.

I did it! I jumped. The fresh powder was delicious underfoot as I skied toward Glen. Together, we glided toward the pristine lower slopes of my favorite run, the backside of Three, and then many miles to the lodge below.

We returned home late the following week, exhausted after a day of racing down mountains and the seven-hour drive. I walked through the house in a daze, feeling as though we had been robbed. From the kitchen, a few pots and pans and some dishes were missing; a desk chair from our library and all the liquor was gone. That night of our return, I told the boys about the separation.

Glen, my stoic young man, looked up at me and said, "I knew it would happen; I felt it coming. Oh, Mom, how will we live without Dad?"

Fourteen-year-old Brad, closest to his father, was more traumatized by the gravity of Bob's leaving. That first night, with heavy heart, I lay next to him on his bed, holding him while he sobbed. "It'll be all right, sweetheart, he'll always be your father and be there for you."

Bob could not stay away. As if by magic, this phantom husband who had been absent most of our 21-year marriage was suddenly there every time I turned around. I would come down the stairs and see him sitting in his favorite chair, reading. I was in mourning while the corpse was still walking around. I told him to go, but he kept coming, until my attorney finally put out a restraining order. After that, he would drive around the neighborhood, and find me as I walked the dog in early evenings, then follow me in the car. I never knew he cared until I wanted to leave.

I thought our divorce was settled amicably. I got the house, and Bob got all the investments and the medical practice. The house I designed and built with money parlayed from our previous homes; the first one purchased with a gift from my father in 1960. I knew he was angry, and I was afraid of him, so I agreed to all his requests. My lawyer told me I was getting screwed financially, that after putting him through medical school, Bob should at least give me enough to live on. I was so eager to end the marriage by then that I foolishly did not listen to him. Several weeks later, I needed cash from our savings to pay legal bills and could not understand when the bank informed me the account had been closed.

I called Bob. "Where did all our savings go?"

"I took the money out to put a down payment on a house for myself and closed the account. I have to live somewhere. You wouldn't want me on the street, would you?"

I called my lawyer and he told me that half of those savings were legally mine. I would need to take Bob to court to get it, and by the time I paid court costs and legal fees, I would not end up with enough to make it worthwhile. In Bob's silent anger, he left me with the house, our two boys, and no savings. The child and spousal support he gave me was not enough to live on.

At last I was free, but without a penny in the bank.

CHAPTER

9

60 Minutes *(Los Angeles, 1982)*

At 9:30 a.m., I was in my garage turning on the ignition to start the car, and the phone rang. I ran back into the kitchen and picked it up.

"I'm calling from *60 Minutes*," the male voice said. He told me they were doing a human-interest segment on the marital relationship of divorced spouses who had supported their husbands and wives through professional school. "I understand you fit this profile," he said. "Can I come out to interview you?"

Caught off guard, I stammered, "I guess so."

"How about tomorrow, at this same time? By the way, we'll pay you if you agree to be on the show."

The slight, 30-ish, pink-faced fellow arrived in a rakish baseball cap, matching brown corduroy pants, yellow shirt, and a crazy dotted tie. I learned they had done their research, and already knew the details of my situation.

"How did you find me?"

"Someone named Merle Miller." *Of course, my old studio mate; Merle knew everyone.* I couldn't give the *60 Minutes* guy a straight answer and hated the thought of talking about my private life in public.

Bob and I had been divorced two years. I had no idea how the TV segment would play out but was intrigued by the project and could use the money, so I made the decision to participate. It sounded like an adventure. The filming was to take place at the Beverly Hills Hotel on Sunset Boulevard. Mike Wallace would be coming to Los Angeles from New York to tape the show and interview us. My only instructions were to wear something conservative and to be on time.

The day of the taping was overcast and rainy. I arrived at the appointed hour but, typical of L.A., could not find a place to park. Circling the hotel, I reluctantly gave the car to an attendant. In my only conservative outfit, a black-skirted suit and high-heeled pumps bought for my father's funeral, I dashed in, flushed, hair straggly from the rain. I was ushered into an icy cold, floral-scented room on the second floor with beige and cream striped wallpaper. The crew was busy setting up. Mike Wallace, in a navy blue suit, came over, shook my hand, introduced himself, and then gathered the other interviewees together to explain the protocol.

"You were each chosen because you represent different fields of endeavor. I'll be asking straightforward questions. Just answer as quickly and simply as you can."

There were five others in the group, all about my age, mid-to-late forties, all attractive. Two were men who had put wives through law and dental school, the remaining were women who had supported husbands through architecture, engineering, and aerospace training, and myself, who had supported one through medical school.

We sat in a semicircle on straight-backed, ornately carved, mahogany chairs upholstered in beige, with nothing in front of us. I felt self-conscious with no table to hide behind.

In his confrontational manner, Wallace wanted to know if we were supportive of our former mates' long training, or if we resented their pursuit of an advanced degree. I could sense the numbness of the group. Wallace was beginning to be invasive into our personal lives, and I suddenly wanted to get the hell out of there but could not pick myself up and run; the cameras were rolling. We were on national TV in front of the world. The show was unrehearsed, off the cuff. Wallace prompted each of us with: "What kind of work did you do to support the two of you during the training period, and did you have children?"

Then he asked each of us, one by one, on the air, the most humiliating question: "Did he leave you for someone else, and who was that other person?" When one is put on the spot, there is no time to invent answers; the truth comes out.

The man with a ruddy complexion and a mop of red hair, whose wife had gone to law school, excused himself, saying he needed to use the restroom.

"Cut! We'll take ten, folks."

He came back flushed, motioned "no" with his head, and then looked down at his feet. I could see moisture in his eyes when he said, "A senior partner at her legal firm." Later, he confessed to me privately that he had thrown up in the bathroom.

The girl in black with long, sandy hair, whose husband is now an engineer, sniffled, then blew her nose and could hardly get the words out. "He left me for his secretary."

The dark-skinned woman with close cropped hair in a smart beige suit, whose husband had been in architecture school, waved her hands in the air, then shot her right fist out as if to sock someone, and said, "A whore he met at church."

The quiet fellow dressed in jeans and a navy blazer with brass buttons, whose wife had been a dental student, told us that she couldn't get enough of her tennis pro. "I was so disgusted; I finally walked out and took our two-year-old daughter with me."

The adorable little brunette with big brown eyes, wearing a cinnamon print dress, was the most disheartening when, biting her nails while tears rolled down her cheeks and her voice cracked, told us that her husband studied at home for his aerospace exam.

The houses were five feet apart in her neighborhood and next door, there was a buxom blonde who always worked in her garden wearing shorts and a halter top. The wife noticed that he loved watching the blonde out the window as he sat at his desk.

The brunette was a buyer at the Broadway department store and stopped at home to get some papers one afternoon. His car was in the driveway, but she couldn't find him anywhere. Worried, she dashed next door to ask the neighbor if she had seen him around. The blonde came to the door in a see-through, pink peignoir with nothing under it, smelling of Chanel No. 5. Behind her, through the crack in the bedroom door, the brunette saw her husband naked, scrambling to get his clothes on.

Embarrassed for each of those vulnerable souls who had come to be part of a TV show, seduced by the adventure and a little cash, I wanted to rush over and give each one a hug. *How could Mike Wallace be so insensitive and ask such humiliating questions?*

When he came to me . . . all those years of waiting for Bob to come home, the degradation of knowing, but not wanting to admit his affairs, and sublimating my passions, plus my enormous fear of him, flooded my thoughts. Guarded, I had the presence of mind to say what I knew to be the only honest answer. "No, he did not leave me; I left him for me."

The twenty-minute segment took two hours to tape. After it was over, the six of us were visibly shaken. Wallace invited us to the flamboyant Polo Lounge for a drink. Silently, we ascended in the elevator as if in a trance.

The walls were covered with silver paper, and above the bar hung gigantic portraits of horses. Mike Wallace sat next to me in the white leather booth. By then I hated him for making us feel like cogs in a wheel with no escape. I ordered Pinot Grigio. He relaxed, loosened his tie, and ordered a vodka tonic. Moving closer, he cornered me:

"You said you're a painter. Do you know my wife, Lorraine Perigord? She's also an artist, in New York, has a studio in SoHo, works like a demon every day and long into the night. I rarely see her. She's obsessed with her work. I think it's brilliant."

My eyes widened, *SoHo, that's where I'd like to be.* I could see by the gleam in his eyes that he loved her deeply. I thought, *perhaps he's a human after all.*

The segment aired the following week, and I watched it with friends. Two months later, I read in *The New York Times* that Mike Wallace's wife left him. I wondered for whom; perhaps for herself?

CHAPTER

10

An Invisible Network of Angels

It had taken me ten years to summon up the audacity to leave Bob, and then I felt guilt and remorse. Several months after he was gone, I finally started to feel the weight lifted and chains removed. Even though I was completely broke, I thanked God each day for my courage and hugged myself: *I've been through a war and I'm still here.*

A robin settled on the edge of the patio, next to the pot of geraniums as the sun blazed. It was 1979; I sat in my Pacific Palisades patio with the *Los Angeles Times* spread out on the round wrought iron table. My eyes scanned the vast green lawn, stretching to the cliff's drop-off, dotted with the yellow and orange marigolds I had planted. On the last page of the classifieds, a tiny two-liner caught my eye: *Wedding locations needed, call Marilyn at #.* I wrestled with myself. *Do I want to prostitute my house? Yes, I need the money.* I immediately went into my kitchen and dialed her up.

Marilyn Jeanette came the next afternoon, her dark hair striking against her all-white pantsuit. We tromped through the yard, and then sat by the pool with iced tea. The location scout breathed in the salty sea air. "What a glorious spot. Sure you want to do this?" I nodded. "Need the money." "I think the center of the railroad ties by the cliff's edge is perfect for the ceremonies. The guests will see the wedding couples against the ocean backdrop, and it'll make great photos." She asked if it was okay to bring couples to visit the following week. A succession of young, middle-aged, and old couples, holding hands, some with their arms folded into one another, came giggling, swooning, or dancing around, all signing up to recite their vows in my greatest work of art, my garden.

The weddings had been taking place for eight months until one Sunday evening at about 10:00 p.m. The night was winding down, caterers cleaning up in the kitchen and grandparents, children, and the bride and groom were dancing the hora. The pink cloths on the round rental tables were laden with ladies' purses and soiled linen napkins. The band's sound system seemed to be getting louder and louder. I was standing in back watching the scene with Marilyn, when I heard the bell and a pounding on the front door.

It was the police. "This your house, lady?"

"Yes, officer; is there a problem?"

"Neighbors are complaining about loud music coming from your yard."

"I'm having a wedding, sir.

"They say you're having weddings every weekend. You got a commercial license?"

"No, sir."

"I'm giving you a warning this time, but any more complaints, and you'll wind up in court."

In my zeal to earn money from the house I had not considered how it would impact my neighbors. I felt ashamed and returned deposits for future bookings. The weddings had to stop.

Several months later I got a call from an old friend and film director, Lou Antonio. "How ya doin' on your own, Elaine? Interested in having a film shoot at your house? I need a location for my new movie with Rock Hudson, *The Star Maker*."

"Of course, and it'll be so good to see you, Lou."

Then, several months after that, Lou told a friend putting together a Jacques Cousteau film about my site. They shot scenes in my pool and down at the ocean from my cliff's edge with a telephoto lens. I felt an invisible network of angels had found me and knew I needed help. My one asset, my home, became my business.

When the money was pouring in, I opened a new savings account, stopped into Dean Witter on Wilshire Boulevard on a whim, and bought a small amount of stock in Fidelity Magellan. I was the only woman in the place. I felt comfortable slipping back into my old painting clothes, and, after driving the boys to school, kept going on to the studio again, painting my hard-edged, figurative portraits of friends. The portraits were amassing, and I started to feel like a real artist. I needed to find a market for them.

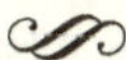

Sixteen people sat around an oval walnut table in a nondescript beige room at 7:00 p.m. on the tenth floor of an office building in the Miracle Mile section of Los Angeles. Calvin Goodman was presenting his art marketing seminar. The attendees were mostly young artists: guys with beards, 23-year-old girls in tie-dye dresses and beads, one older bald art dealer, and 46-year-old me, eagerly taking copious notes. Our common goal was to make a living in the art world, hoping to be somebody someday. I sat next to a thin, dark-haired, would-be art dealer named John Bolen who was planning to set up a new gallery near my Venice studio. At the end of the twelve sessions, John leaned over and asked if he could come by and see my work.

It was on an overcast day, the studio dark and my lights insufficient, when John came as arranged. Nevertheless, he studied each painting, and then sat down on my paint spattered stool. "Think those people you painted will buy their portraits?"

"Perhaps."

"I'd like to plan a show."

Giddy with excitement, I almost knocked him over, shaking his hand. My invitation list included everyone I knew. My models brought their husbands, children and parents to the opening. Throngs stuffed the new small gallery, spilling into the street. Susan Anthony's husband bought the painting of his wife lounging in a sexy pink negligee, and dear Linda bought her own portrait in a red robe, to hang over their grand piano. Lorie Long bought her daughter's portrait for their grandmother, and Tony Segundo bought my sketch of his wife. It was a Saturday afternoon happening in the sleepy town of Venice, California. John Bolen sold like crazy and was ecstatic with his fifty percent commission.

I was inspired to start making other proposals. The Brand Municipal Gallery in Glendale, east of Los Angeles, was showing emerging artists. I sent slides of the portraits I had remaining, and they accepted me. The space was vast, with high ceilings and a grand entrance at the end of a tree lined path. Few friends came because of the distance, but when strangers crowded around and admired my work, I felt proud and professional.

Back in the studio, my life was at last on track, and I started painting dancers flying through the air to reflect my new freedom. I was not pleased with the first paintings and rubbed the pigment down, leaving a trace. Then, when they dried, I worked on them again, and something amazing happened. The colors from underneath showed through the canvas, creating a subtle softness, a translucent effect. I continued rubbing and waiting between coats, and within several weeks I had developed a new experimental technique. I painted one, two, and then three people flying together through the air, holding hands. The paintings had great force, and with each layer of pigment the luminosity increased. I called this new group of paintings my *Synergistic Series.* Cindy was in college, and my boys were involved with sports and doing well in school. I was suddenly fulfilling my dream and the adrenalin was flowing.

CHAPTER

11

Erotic Series

It had been over a year and Zack was still painting in my studio on Friday afternoons. We shared stories while eating lunch at Hal's in our paint-strewn clothes. We found that several of our ancestors had come from the same area of Russia, and then he opened up with his own marital problems.

"My marriage has been floundering for years and you've given me the courage to do something about it. I'm filing for a separation."

"No, please don't do that," I said. "Not because of me."

"Being around you has helped me to realize that I should have done it years ago."

In the months that followed, after he left his wife, Zack moved out of his family home, into a small house he bought in a nearby area and set up his own art studio. On afternoons too beautiful to be inside, we met in Santa Monica's park overlooking the ocean, and listened to the crashing waves. I brought chicken sandwiches and he, the wine. As strangers strolled by, we lay in each other's arms, oblivious to the world around us. He had become my best friend and mentor with whom I could share everything.

On a whim, we grabbed a few clothes one day and jumped on a flight for San Francisco to see *La Traviata*. The following month, we drove up the coast, north of San Francisco, to Sea Ranch. We stopped along the way in Calistoga, where we sunk down in the sulfur-smelling mud baths at Dr. Wilkinson's Hot Springs Resort and laughed ourselves silly. Each day I ran to my small studio and painted with frenzy. I felt that an artist's work should reflect her life, and mine was, for the first time, mired in sexual desire. It was as though I had been asleep, suddenly to awaken as this highly charged sexual being. My new paintings were the embodiment of the new me.

I had always painted from real life, but the new series necessitated that I research photographic imagery, giving reference for my new subtly abstract work, which became more sensual as time progressed. Each painting consisted of six, sometimes eight layers of pigment, allowing the colors from beneath to shine through. The moving, intertwined figurative forms exuded love and spirit. Classical music flowed out of my ten-dollar radio in the corner as I danced in the dim studio with the door open and the black iron gate locked. I was on a great high, wildly in love, and painted about it. Those images were Zack's and my offspring. As I finished one, I started another, sometimes working on three and four at a time.

I kept pinching myself; "Could this be real?" I was sure it was meant to be. Relentless in his demands for my time, the phone rang many times a day with him on the other end.

I became addicted, communicating my glow through the new sensual paintings. Bob was always uncomfortable showing his feelings; now I was hearing words of love daily from Zack. Those words infect one's brain, and yet there were dark days when I feared nirvana could not last forever. He had heroically saved my life; surely, he would never abandon me.

After we had been together for five years, Zack visited his children one evening and, expecting him at his house, I called to say good

night. He did not answer. I called again, and then realized he must have stayed all night with his family. He confessed the next day.

"When I go home my wife begs me to stay; she cries about our separation, wants me to come back."

I was overcome with pain in my gut. Holding my aching belly, I said, "What can I say? You need to do what your heart tells you."

A few days later, when I hadn't heard from him, I called again to say good night and there was no answer. The next day he called and wanted to see me. Of course I saw him, and again at night when I called, he was away. Immobilized, I stoically laid in bed staring at the ceiling, not moving. It was in the white bedroom overlooking the azure Pacific I had hoped would heal my marriage, and in the same bed Rock Hudson had shared with Suzanne Pleshette in *The Star Maker* film. I stayed in that bed for days, weeks.

Don't answer the phone, Elaine. Don't see him. Walk away, now. But I couldn't, I didn't. He had become my life.

A raw, gut emotion finally erupted when I realized he was trying to hold on to both of us. It's easy to see what I should have done in retrospect. In my anguish, I could not work or sleep. My fear of losing the one person who thought me lovable, and whom I believed had saved me, crashed down. I had been functioning so well as a productive adult, but the sleeplessness and stress intensified my grief, manifesting into a rage I had sublimated my entire marriage. Whenever Zack questioned doing the right thing by leaving his wife, my hysterical wrath ultimately clarified his decision to go back to her.

Heartsick, the remorse and agony of my loss would not leave me.

CHAPTER

12

The German

I had to get away. It was 1980, and I was alone in the Pacific Palisades house. My youngest son, Brad, had started college. At the first opportunity, I dashed off to New York City and stayed at a bed and breakfast in an apartment at the NYU Silver Towers. A twenty-foot Picasso sculpture faced the entrance, which I took as a positive sign. On my first day I took the subway uptown to the Museum of Modern Art and made a pact with myself not to speak with any man who was not wearing a suit and tie. Zack had refused to dress up. I knew it was silly, but in my attempt to heal my broken heart I made a game of it.

At lunchtime in the cafeteria, I spotted a hefty fellow in his sixties with gray-brown hair, in tweed, seated at the end of a long table in the corner. With my tray in hand, I sat two chairs away from him and finally asked if he was here from out of town.

"*Ja, Frankfurt, Deutschland.*"

"You must be an art lover." He told me he was on the Board of the Frankfurt museum.

"I'm an artist, here to see the shows," I said. We chatted about the art scene in New York, and he asked if I was familiar with the galleries. "Most are down in SoHo. You should see them while you're in New York."

He asked me how far away SoHo was and offered to pay me to take him.

"Wouldn't think of it," I said, as I stood up, our lunch finished. "Come on, we'll grab a cab, and be downtown before rush hour."

Walter Greisner and I spent the next three hours wandering into and ducking out of the galleries on West Broadway, Spring, and Prince Streets, discussing the paintings, until he spoke up. "I need to go back to the Park Lane Hotel and get off my feet," he said in his broken English. "I'm here alone; would you be so kind as to join me for dinner?"

I thanked him and said I was busy, even though I had no plans.

"How about tomorrow?" he said. "I leave the following day." When he said that, realizing how bright and interesting he was, I told him I'd be happy to join him.

"I know a great little Italian place near your hotel, Isle of Capri, on 61st and Third. Let's meet there at 7:00."

He was already there when I arrived. His eyes lit up, and he waved when he saw me searching the room. We chatted about his wife, Ann-Marie, their three children and his home in Sachsenhausen, a suburb of Frankfurt. He told me he was on his way to Los Angeles to see the new Temporary Contemporary Museum and staying in Santa Monica at the Miramar Hotel.

"That's right between my home and studio."

"Then I must see your paintings while I'm there."

"Yes, I hope so."

The following week I returned home, excited about the art I had seen in New York and anxious to get back to work. I had let Walter know the date and time I would be back, and when I arrived, keys in hand, he was standing at the door to my studio.

"Hi stranger, come on in," I said as I unlatched the gate and turned the lights on, directing him to sit in my model's chair. He seemed larger now, and his suit and tie out of place in casual Venice.

"How about a cup of tea?"

"*Ja, vielen Dank.*"

I watched him peruse the studio, following his eyes as they glanced at my canvases of the Synergistic Series, in my new rubbed technique.

"Do you have more of these, with the people leaping in the air?"

"Of course," I said as I started bringing others out, and then he noticed one of the sensual paintings of bodies embracing.

"Woo, that one's magnificent. Can I see it?"

No one had seen these paintings. They were my secret stash, still tacky from the linseed and stand oils used to add luster, the subtle odor still permeating the room. I brought one out at a time and returned each to the rack before bringing the next.

"The way you've applied the pigment is unique. Colors from underneath are luminous. Someday I'd like to introduce you to art dealers in Frankfurt." With added respect, he said, "You mentioned you also make serigraphs."

"Yes, I print in my garage at home. If you want to see them, I'll run you over."

After another hour in the studio, I drove over to my house, ten minutes away. We went directly into my garage where I had my silkscreen studio. The air was thick with fumes from the xylene solution I used to clean the screens. I opened the flat files and he went through them on his own as I climbed the steps into the kitchen and brought back a glass of Chablis. I was handing it to him as he pulled out a print of a brilliant sun, looming behind dark cumulus clouds, reflecting on the ocean below.

"This one's my favorite, it's so serene," he said.

I immediately grabbed it, scrawled my signature and the date in the lower right corner, and rolled it up before he could utter a word. I secured it with a rubber band and handed it back to him. "Here, take this home to Ann-Marie; maybe she'll frame it."

"*Vielen Dank* . . . she'll love it."

We left the garage without Walter ever entering the house. I didn't dare distract him from the art. Within an hour, we were driving back to his rental car parked in front of my studio.

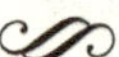

I thought about Walter's response to my Synergistic and Erotic series, and within the week I had slides of the paintings made, and sent proposals to several art dealers. The Downey Museum, one half hour east of downtown Los Angeles, was the first to respond, with offerings of a one-person exhibition. I spent the following eight months preparing. The day before the opening, my old friend Joy Nuell, who had her own radio news show, called to say she could not make the reception, but suggested we do an interview on the phone. She would run it the following day, and it would repeat every twenty minutes all day, from 7:00 a.m. to 7:00 p.m.

"The Downey Museum's so courageous to show my Erotic Series of paintings," I said, "and the opening's tomorrow night from 7 to 9."

January 9, 1981 was a crisp, cold night in Downey, but inside the large white structure, it was packed to capacity and steamy hot. Uncle Morry and Aunt Florence gulped with embarrassment as they walked through the gallery viewing the paintings, and the DeMayos from next door in the Palisades could not look me in the eye. I smiled demurely and thanked everyone for coming but could not wait to get out of there.

At 8:00 a.m. the next morning, a frantic call came from the

chairman of the Museum Board. "We're closing your show down. It's not fit for family viewing. Get over here as fast as you can."

I dashed across town to East Los Angeles through Civic Center traffic from Pacific Palisades on the freeway and arrived at 10:00 to face a bevy of white trucks with NBC, CBS and ABC inscribed on the sides. The front door to the museum was covered with brown paper, on which was scrawled:

> ***EXHIBITION CLOSED TO ALL PERSONS UNDER 18.***
> ***Use side entrance, ID required.***

I kept reminding myself not to get hysterical.

I found out later that none of the Board members had actually seen the show, but several had heard Joy's newscast and were horrified. After much discussion, we decided to put the entire show in the back room and replace it with a new exhibition of my paintings. I ran home, and piled the portraits left from the Bolen Gallery exhibition into my station wagon and brought them out the following day. Any adult wanting to see the Erotic Series could ask the attendant and be escorted to the back room. Nightly TV news and all the newspapers carried the story, with five articles in the *L.A. Times* alone.

It was an exciting time for me. Calls wanting to show the work came in from private galleries, not restricted by a board or town policies. I went with a small gallery in Laguna Beach and thankfully, there were no repercussions.

During that same period, Walter Greisner was writing me letters, telling me he had a long list of art dealers he wanted me to meet in Frankfurt. I was too busy and kept putting him off, but finally consented to make the trip.

The brooding dark skies threatened rain as my Lufthansa Airlines flight landed at the Frankfurt airport. Walter was waiting for me in baggage claim, his blue Mercedes motor still running by the curb. We drove up the winding roads of his residential area called Sachsenhausen and stopped in front of an elementary school. Children were in the yard tossing balls, and the German flag hung high on the pole.

"This whole beautiful area was Jewish before the war," he said, "and when Hitler's men rounded up the neighborhood, this school is where they held everyone, until trucks took them off to the camps."

Suddenly, I felt that I had to be careful with what I said. *Walter was obviously not Jewish. I wondered if he knew that I was.*

That old fear I remembered as a child during the early 1940s reemerged. Between the ages of five and eleven, when the Second World War was taking place, I remember one Passover my grandma Sonia, in her broken English, saying, "Elainie dear, run over and pull the window shades down. We don't want the neighbors to see our Seder table."

My parents were quiet and secretive. They did not talk about the Holocaust, but I sensed we were living in alien territory; an ominous fear always haunted us.

As we arrived at Walter's home, Ann-Marie, an ample *Frau* with long golden hair pulled up in a bun, was waiting for us by the front door. She grabbed my hands and kissed both cheeks, then led me into the house. We entered the dining room first, where my silkscreen print had been framed and prominently hung over the buffet.

"See, here it is, we love it!" Then she ran into the kitchen and reemerged with a platter of cheeses and meats as Walter opened beers for all of us. Knowing I loved the opera, they had gotten tickets to take me to see *Macbeth* that very evening. However, the flight from Los Angeles had been eleven hours and hard as I tried, I was embarrassed that I could not stay awake.

For the next three days, Walter and I went from gallery to gallery as he introduced me to art dealers he had known over the years. After that, we left Frankfurt and drove the Autobahn to Kronberg, a nearby hillside village with narrow streets and quaint little shops. Our destination was the Satyra gallery, which specialized in erotic paintings. It was a serious small space, run by a handsome, dark-haired art dealer in her fifties, wearing an elegant black suit. She responded favorably to my slides and the small painting I brought. We planned for me to send her several larger works to show in the gallery. As we walked out, cupping his hand over his mouth, Walter whispered, "She's a Jew, came back after the war."

Then he said he wanted to show me something he thought I would find interesting. We drove down the hill and arrived at the Kronberg Castle, built of rocks in 1230, beside Altkoenig Mountain. We walked through the fine old structure in hushed tones.

Walter pulled me aside and again whispered, "This is where Hitler hid out during the Holocaust when he had death threats. It was the Kronberg family home before the Nazis took it over."

I clutched the banister to hold myself up, then turned away so he could not see my expression.

The following year, I had my first exhibition in Frankfurt at Das Bilderhaus Gallery on Hermannstrasse in the new section of the city.

"Here, stand in front and they'll crowd around for your lecture," said the dealer.

"They're expecting it; we do this at every opening."

A standing crowd filled the gallery, except for a few older folks sequestered on benches at the sides. The invitation had said 5:00 p.m., and at five sharp, I was instructed to start my talk. I spoke about the silkscreen process, demonstrating how I piled the oil-based inks of each color on one side of the squeegee and other hues next to them, swishing back and forth, slowly blending to create a sunset effect called "split fountain." I had brought a small silkscreen and many similar-sized French archival papers, and then ran off fifteen to twenty prints, handing them out to the guests. The audience was excited to be able to bring home a work of art and did not seem to mind that I spoke in English.

At 7:00 o'clock, Walter and Ann-Marie waved their good-byes, as I followed the crowd downstairs into the basement of the gallery. The walls were painted blue and were cluttered with paintings from artists who had shown in the gallery. In the corner, a live combo played jazz and old show tunes.

The pianist stopped playing and started singing "God Bless America" when she saw me come in. Beer, schnitzel, and crudités were passed around, and cheeses filled a tray on the bar. Most of the guests were other artists in their thirties and forties. Swept up in the frivolity, I sang along with them as I consumed my beer, and in their presence, I felt all my anxieties melt away. It was as though I had stumbled into their special, private world. Some came over, introducing themselves, wanting to know about the galleries in America. The next day the phone rang with invitations to visit two artists' studios, and a tall, good-looking banker I had met invited me for dinner. Thus began my affection for Frankfurt and its art community.

Several months later, I took the eleven-hour flight to Frankfurt again, this time on my own. I stayed at a bed and breakfast in the old section and saw Walter, Ann-Marie, and my new friends, then finalized details for a more serious exhibition of my large oil paintings.

Returning home to Los Angeles, I packed my Synergistic and Erotic series together in a huge 50″ x 65″ x 4′ wood crate and shipped them by sea for a six-week journey to the Galerie Woeller Paquet. I planned to stay in Europe exploring galleries in other cities during the exhibition, and then return to Frankfurt to see that the unsold paintings were shipped back in good order.

I wanted to rent my house out during this period to help pay for my trips, and was lucky to find Annie Constantinesco, a real estate broker who specialized in the film industry. She found me a summer tenant named Maurice Jarre who needed a home with a piano. He had produced the musical scores for *Doctor Zhivago* and *Lawrence of Arabia*, and won the Academy Award for both. Now he was working on *A Passage to India*.

A handsome, convivial, gray-haired Frenchman in his late fifties walked in on the day of my departure with his svelte Asian girlfriend Fong as I was frantically transferring clothes from the bedroom closet into my office. They immediately pitched in, and we continued emptying the closet as if they were family.

The exhibition at Woeller Paquet was held in the venerable old section across the Main River of Frankfurt on Schneckenhofstrasse, and was more sophisticated than the Das Bilderhaus show. The lecture I gave beforehand was briefer, with no beer hall downstairs. In its place, black-tie waiters served champagne. The guests wore furs, boots, and jewels, and people I did not know from Switzerland and Germany surprised me by buying my paintings. Friends I had met the previous year attended. After the show, we went to an old pub for dinner, where again we sang and the beer flowed.

I left the group and returned to my room at the bed and breakfast but, in my excitement, sleep eluded me. The night was frigid, and the heat was off at that late hour. I sat up and wrapped myself in the down comforter from the bed; tears came to my eyes. I felt so lucky. After all those years of yearning to be an artist, I could never have predicted the actual experience of that evening. I felt that exhibitions were usually a letdown after all the preparation and had the urge to share my thoughts with my young sister, Debbie, a budding artist. I grabbed a sheet of stationery and jotted off a letter, ending it with: "The exhibition at the end does not compare with the challenge and joy of creating the art."

While the show was in progress, I took the train to Berlin, lined up another exhibition on Pariser Strasse with my prints, and spent time in the bleak Eastern sector (before the wall came down). I went on to Greece and Turkey, and when I returned to Frankfurt to oversee the packing, I discovered a painting had been stolen. It was the smallest in the show, 24″ x 36″, but my favorite. I was devastated.

I returned home six weeks later as our contract had specified, having confirmed the date and time with Maurice, and no one was there. I wandered through my home in a daze. A synthesizer lay on the living room floor near the piano, and sheet music covered every possible surface. It was obvious that the musical score was nowhere near completion. After I waited for hours, Maurice and Fong casually walked in, oblivious to our contract and my planned arrival. They were so special, and the score was obviously not finished; I could not ask them to leave. Displaced in my own home, we sat at the kitchen table to discuss the situation and agreed that I would stay downstairs in the room off the kitchen for as long as it took to finish the score.

I don't remember how long it took, but when the score was

completed, I was pleased that I had endured the inconvenience. I watched the Academy Awards that year at home, and when they announced the names for the best musical score, after showing clips from all the films nominated, the announcer said, "The envelope, please." A starlet pranced up to the mike, opened the envelope and said, "Maurice Jarre, for *A Passage to India*." I was bursting with pride.

I was drawn back to Frankfurt on the pretext of finding the stolen painting. Actually, I loved being there. They were aware of the world around them, and the friends I made in Frankfurt offered me something I had never experienced, and unknowingly yearned for. No one there knew where I came from, my ex-husband or the home I lived in. They responded to my work and to me personally. Their enthusiasm gave me a new and heightened feeling of self worth.

I was fortunate that one of my new friends wanted to sublet her apartment for a month. It was a cozy one-bedroom near the *Zeil*, a walking street with cafes, theaters and shops in the center of town. I reconnected with my new friends and, when alone, sat in a cafe sipping coffee, watching couples stroll arm in arm in their simple but substantial clothing.

Woeller Paquet, my art dealer, recommended an attorney, and said he was a good friend, a Harvard man, who would help me find the stolen painting. The lawyer was about 50, an American from Vermont with pale skin, silver-blond hair, and what appeared to be a small basketball under his white shirt and windbreaker. He suggested we go to dinner to discuss the case and picked me up at the apartment in his shiny, gray Volvo. That Sunday afternoon, it was cool and overcast. We drove the Autobahn to a quaint restaurant with checkered cloths on the tables, overlooking the River Main. Between bites of Wiener schnitzel, sauerkraut and mugs of beer, he laid out a plan to find the painting. He seemed like a gentleman and was totally professional.

On our way back to Frankfurt, Mozart was serenading from his tape deck as we barreled along at a high speed on the Autobahn. All of a sudden, he reached over, his hand groping, trying to pull me closer. I instinctively recoiled. Cars were whizzing by. The whole incident happened so fast. I moved closer to the door. He sped up, and then reached way over again, grabbing my breast.

"Please don't," I screamed, as I glanced at the speedometer. It read 250 kph, which I calculated to be 155 mph. I gasped.

"Watch where you're going!" I looked up and saw the Frankfurt offramp sign. *Thank god we're almost back.* He remained in the middle lane as we drove past the exit.

"Where are we going?"

"My place."

"Please, I need to get back."

He kept driving in the middle lane at high speed. We approached the next offramp and he was still grabbing at me, moving at high speed. I was trying to figure out how to climb into the back seat when I noticed the car veering into the turn-off lane, finally exiting up the Griesheim ramp. As the car came to a stop at the top of the hill, I opened the door and bolted out, clutching my purse, as cars whizzed by. I had no idea where I was. It appeared to be an industrial area, void of humans.

He opened the passenger window and yelled, "Get back in the car; you don't know where you are." I ducked behind a parked car. He passed me, then made a U-turn, and came back around. He got out of the car and started running after me. I ducked again into a clump of bushes and sat on the ground with my head down in fetal position. He didn't see me. I watched him walk back to the car and slowly drive away.

As I started walking, I tripped in deep mud, and then moved

over to the street, where it was easier to walk in my high heels. There were no street lamps. It was isolated and dark. I thought I saw a figure off in the distance, but when I arrived, no one was there. It was early November and a blast of cold wind rushed through me. Thankfully, I had worn a sweater and jacket. I must have walked an hour searching for an open store, a house with lights, phone kiosk, or any place to call Walter or a taxi.

Headlights approached from behind going very slowly. *My God, who could that be?* I jumped out of the street and with the light, glanced at my watch; it read 10:18. The car pulled up beside me. It was the attorney, rolling down the window and yelling, "Want a ride back?"

Leaning over, he opened the door. I kept walking. "No, I'm fine."

"I promise I won't bother you."

"No, thank you."

"You're a long way from home." The car rolled along beside me as I walked. "Come on, it's late."

"Only if I can sit in the back."

"Get in."

CHAPTER

13

Third Street Promenade

Married women of my generation anticipated eventual security, not being on our own in a panic to survive. In the fifties, sixties and seventies, men took care of their women, even discouraged them from going out alone at night. I had planned to be married until I died.

By 1986, Zack was back with his wife and Bob was in his new house, four miles up the road. Before the women's movement in the late fifties, around the time of my marriage, Henry Miller, in *The Tropic of Cancer*, referred to women as "stupid cunts." We received little respect, except as sex objects, housekeepers, teachers, and secretaries. The women's movement was a "stand up and fight" response.

After the weddings in my garden were halted, my children each got summer jobs, and I was lucky to get a position teaching the serigraphic process at UCLA. The day I learned that I had gotten the job, I called my friend Ed Wenner to share my elation. Ed was the father of Jann Wenner who started *Rolling Stone* magazine in New York and had recently shared his pride about that with us. Ed's business was putting property deals together. Bob and I had invested with his group, and as a gift he gave us a subscription to the magazine. When Bob and I separated, Ed and I had continued our friendship as ski buddies.

He thanked me for calling and said there was something

he wanted to show me, suggesting that we go for breakfast. This sounded intriguing. I liked Ed, thought he was brilliant, and having breakfast with him would be a welcome diversion from my studio isolation.

The early morning beach fog was clearing and the sun starting to warm the air. Ed rang my doorbell wearing ironed Levis, Gucci loafers, and a Ralph Lauren polo shirt. He was a short man with straight brown hair and smelled of Old Spice and Listerine. We sat outside in the patio by the fire pit at Boulangerie on Main Street, a Tyrolean style bakery in Ocean Park. After our scrambled eggs and croissants, he said, "Feel like taking a walk? I want your feedback on an idea I've been mulling around."

We headed toward Santa Monica along Main and over to Third Street. J.C. Penney's was the only property still maintained in the area. The rest of the street was filled with potholes and rundown old buildings in disrepair, with "for sale" and "foreclosure" notices pasted to the front doors. Drugged, homeless souls were lying against the structures.

"We're here. Let's sit down," Ed said. He sat down on the curb next to an overflowing trash can. I joined him, our feet resting in the gutter.

"I've had a dream about this area for years," Ed said, and told me his vision of buying up the old buildings. Most of them were in foreclosure and could be purchased for low prices. He would need to get a variance to make the area into a walking street but was sure it was possible. His dream was to hire architects and landscapers and ultimately have a mall with theaters, shops and restaurants. He had researched it and knew it was possible.

"L.A. needs a place for folks to hang out. Everyone's so isolated in their homes and cars," he said. "This could be like the *Zeil* in Frankfurt or St. Stephen's Square in Vienna, with sidewalk cafes and musicians entertaining."

We agreed; it would revolutionize the community. He got up off the curb, enthusiastically waving his hands as he charted his plan.

"Why don't you go in with me? You're the perfect partner, with your experience in art and design."

"Oh Ed, I'd love to, but I don't have the kind of money you're talking about. Bob wiped out our savings."

"I thought there might be some way. We could have such fun planning it."

As we walked back, we stopped in front of each building with a foreclosure sign, peeking in the windows. Most were stately old structures, some of brick, others with Mexican tiles on the floor. Visualizing them renovated and painted, the project took on a whole new light.

We walked back to Boulangerie, and I bought a loaf of sourdough. In the car, Ed said, "You think I'm crazy, don't you?"

"No. Just a wild dreamer wanting to improve the world. I wish I had the means to join you."

That night I could not get Ed's dream out of my head. At 4:00 a.m., I finally got up, thinking back to Henry Miller's description of women and said to myself, *Elaine, you're not a stupid cunt; you are on your own now. No one's going to take care of you. You had better figure out how to take care of yourself. Teaching that one class at UCLA is not going to get back your savings for emergencies.*

I brewed a cup of coffee and, scanning the business section of the *L.A. Times,* I noticed banks advertising new low mortgage rates. The idea resonated. In my nightgown and robe, I shuffled through my steel box of important documents, and found the original mortgage agreement. We were paying nine and a half percent interest. I remembered how hard it was for Bob to get a loan on our tenuous cliff property, lucky to get any at all, even at that high rate. I mulled the subject over in my mind for several days, then called the bank.

The following week, I was sitting in First Nationwide's wood-paneled office in my black suit. This was all new to me. I was an artist and a mother, not a businesswoman. Artists don't like to deal with money, but I needed to learn. By the time I left the bank, I had refinanced the house at six percent, lowering my monthly payments, and taken out enough cash to invest a sizable chunk in Ed Wenner's dream project, Third Street Promenade in Santa Monica.

Unfortunately, Ed died before the project was completed, but his daughter took over, and his legacy lives on in that crowded, intensely active walking street, teeming with bookstores, sidewalk cafes and fine restaurants, three multiplex movie theaters, and all the latest chain stores on the lower levels of our office and apartment buildings. It became a magnet for meeting friends and people-watching. I continue to receive quarterly checks from the investment, and when I walk through the three-block promenade, I swell with pride that I helped make Ed Wenner's dream become more than a reality; it became a phenomenon.

CHAPTER

14

New York City

I watched the people in line at the Public Theater on Lafayette next door to my new loft as I waited for the moving van to arrive from L.A. Faint voices of a chorus could be heard rehearsing in the theater's basement, sweetening the air, as throngs raced home from work amid windy blasts of magenta, orange and saffron leaves. It was late September 1988, and I was 53. The fall colors were early that year. My shoes crunched the leaves as I ushered the crew into the large brick building and up the elevator to my second floor loft.

"Hey lady, where do you want this load?"

"Let's put the desk and boxes in the far corner and the easel in the center of the room. The blank canvases go against the wall."

"This all you've got for this immense space?"

"That's all, boys." And they were gone.

As soon as they drove away, I realized my television never arrived. I thought, *Who needs a TV anyway? I'm in New York City, the center of the universe.*

I wandered through my new 4400-square-foot home, delighted with myself for finding such a good deal. The windows faced the street, with the vast inner area essentially dark, except for a horizontal window over the sink. In the far rear left corner, there was a small room looking out onto a shaft and an old mattress folded up on the floor. *Great*, I thought, while brushing off the dust and making the bed, *I won't have to sleep on the hard floor.*

I was excited, young, and reborn. The spacious whitewashed walls looked bare without any art. I visualized my paintings hanging, sorry not to have shipped work. *I'll need to make new ones*, I thought. *I'll fill the walls; it will be my temporary gallery.*

Around the corner I found a deli and brought back a pizza for dinner, eggs and tea for breakfast. I toppled into bed as soon as the sun went down, oblivious to the grime and mold in the darkened room.

My dreams were of an earthquake, not unusual for this Angeleno. I was awakened by a faint rumbling, my jar of lotion jumping around and then falling over. Tossing and turning, I felt the floor begin to shake. The reverberation increased and became more intense.

Switching on the hanging light, I saw that my watch read 4:00 a.m. What was going on? Was it my imagination, my fatigue? An odor of diesel fumes emanating from the floor vents reached my nostrils. Bolting upright from the mattress, my red hair askew, in my old tan sweats and bare feet, I dashed to the front windows. The sky was dark, the city still asleep. Trash trucks were filing out, one by one, from a garage beneath my building. I could not believe what I was seeing. I had wanted to live downtown near other artists and just paint.

After twenty minutes, the rumbling stopped. The trucks were all out, but the fumes hung low in my enormous space. Slowly, I ambled back to bed and dropped down on the mattress, the dust flying up with a poof.

The question I pondered, as I lay sleepless was, *do I stay in this giant loft and endure the gases and rumbles at dawn, or do I get out immediately and search the city again for a big place I can afford?* I understood why the price was so low. I was in too much of a hurry to settle down. Before I found this loft, I had my eye on another one in SoHo on Broome, snapped up before I could open my checkbook, even though they had promised it to me. That was a harsh awakening to the trauma of finding a good place to live and work in Manhattan.

I waited until 9:00 a.m., then walked to the corner public phone and called my real estate broker. He gently calmed me.

"Don't worry, darling, of course you can break your lease, considering the problem. Pick you up at noon."

My short, stocky broker with a black ponytail and horn-rimmed glasses took my hands in his. "I know how you loved that loft; you must be devastated." He said, "Don't fret, my dear, we'll find you another wonderful place."

The shine of the previous day had turned to gloom. A gentle rain was falling, and I realized I did not even own an umbrella. We climbed into his metallic blue 1986 Fiat and disappeared into the midday traffic, horns blowing and sirens screaming. I glanced down at the flood of black umbrellas as we slowly made our way farther downtown. We passed Houston Street and he said, "I have an appointment at just the place for you," as he turned east on Prince.

"Where are you going? I told you SoHo. We're going in the opposite direction."

"You'll see; it's a good place, renovated building; there was a fire, it's all new now. Slightly away from the SoHo action, but close enough."

We arrived at the corner of Prince and Bowery, a five story gray, concrete block building with a black iron fence and gate, creating a pocket sized courtyard; Number 2 Prince Street. After we rode up the elevator to the top floor, the door opened into a small, but bright immaculate space with high ceilings, one third the size of the Lafayette Street loft. The price was the same. The kitchen smelled of fresh paint and had a low wall consisting of a stove, sink and fridge, all shiny and new. A corner building, bathed in light, it had high windows on three sides. Suddenly, the clouds lifted and brilliant sun shone through. It felt right.

The living room, with its profusion of light and natural wood floors, made a perfect art studio, and the dining area became my living room. I bought a small TV for the built-in shelves and ordered a sofa bed from Jennifer's to face it. A standard double mattress and box spring from Sleepy's and a lamp filled the bedroom. That was all I needed.

The first few nights in the apartment were magical; I put on music and danced in the clean open space. At night, the rear red lights from cars moving uptown on Bowery created a rosy glow and the colors of the Chrysler building in the distance illuminated the sky. It seemed as though I was on a vacation. Pinching myself, I said, "No, I'm not going back next week, I'm staying two years."

From my vantage point in Little Italy, I explored the City, and found SoHo to be a ten minute walk. The intensity of the metropolis became my aphrodisiac.

It was early October and the beginning of the art season. On a Saturday afternoon, determined to see what was new, I made my way into SoHo. The 420 West Broadway building was teeming with activity; there were openings on every floor. Sonnabend was showing Jeff Koons's abstract objects and Castelli's gallery was exhibiting Roy Lichtenstein's huge furniture works in Ben-Day dot patterns. I was awed by the size of the works but not impressed with the subject matter, thinking both to be without passion and contrived.

I wore one of my favorite outfits that first day, a green and white print wrap dress with white sandals, perfect for a fall day in Los Angeles. However, I was in New York now, and stood out like a neon light in a sea of darkness. Everyone was wearing black leather over black jeans with black boots. I snuck out meekly, realizing this was a new world and I had yet to learn the language.

Coming back to my apartment, I often landed in the same little Italian restaurant down the block called Ray's. It was close, cheap, and had the best manicotti I had ever tasted, served with house wine and a salad for $5.95. The large back table was filled with a coterie of older men, and their wives of similar age sat nearby. Sometimes at my small table in front, strangers would join me. I learned this was a Mafia hangout, and that John Gotti's obscure, wood-faced clubhouse was across the street. I had not heard of Gotti in Los Angeles, and Mafia was only a word in the news. There was one man in the group with short-cropped, dark wavy hair and intense brown eyes, younger than the others, always watching me. I saw him often in the neighborhood, and he finally introduced himself as Tony Desario. He seemed out of place. His clothes were the latest style. I found him intelligent, but not aware of world events during the past few years. My guess was that he had just been released from prison. He sat next to me at Ray's often at lunch, but always ate dinner with what he called "the family," the Mafia family.

I wandered across the street from the apartment to the Martini restaurant supply house on Bowery, hoping to find a cart for my paints and brushes. The cement floor and green walls were filled with steel sinks, piles of silverware, pots and pans, and a full range of commercial kitchen equipment. Marching up the stairs, I found the perfect aluminum rolling cart for my art supplies, plus Mr. Martini sitting in his office, facing my building. He smiled.

"So happy to finally meet you, I've been watching you from my window," he said in his gruff Italian dialect. "If you ever have a break in or problems, lean out the window and shout. I'll come."

I started noticing, in early mornings on the southwest corner under my windows, a heavyset, middle-aged man with gray hair, in brown tweed and a baseball cap. Each day it was the same. I hid next to the window, behind the wall, to watch. Occasionally, boys would approach, handing him money in exchange for something small. He disappeared for a week, then came back wearing a gray fisherman's hat and a black coat. Sometimes girls and often older, well-dressed couples would hand him money in exchange for something he fished out of his backpack. I surmised he was selling drugs. Never having been exposed to crime in my sheltered life, I called the police.

"There's a drug dealer on my corner, officer. I've been watching him for weeks."

"You sure, lady? This is Mafia territory and if they found out you were watching them, you could be in real trouble."

"What kind of trouble?"

"Let's just say, you should get the hell out of town if you want to stay alive and lay low until this blows over." No one had ever threatened my life before.

"You mean I should leave the city?"

"Yes, you're living in the midst of them, and it's unsafe for you if I shut down their drug ring."

I felt Mr. Martini's eyes on me, sure he had seen me through all those windows, watching the drug dealer. I was living in a fishbowl.

I hung up, called American Airlines and grabbed a flight for L.A. the next morning. I had a tenant in my house, so I called my mom. "Could you pick me up from LAX tomorrow afternoon? I'll explain when I see you."

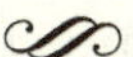

Los Angeles was as though I had never left. There was the shock of sameness: everyone in their cars, the jammed freeways, and the interminable sunshine. I saw my close friends, realizing one never loses a friend when moving away; we only gain new ones. Each day, I made my way from my mother's house in Westwood to my studio in Venice, kept to store my paintings with the intention of returning in two years. I sat at the old steel desk and stared at my work from the past ten years. The reminiscent whiff of oil paint and turpentine still permeated the air. My Erotic Series, inspired by my affair with Zack was, I thought, as good as anything I had seen in New York. I wanted to pack them up and ship them east, but knew I would need to hide them. I did not want to be known as an erotic artist or tempted to continue with that series. I had to expand.

Time passed slowly and I became restless. It was not that I disliked L.A., it was the intensity of New York that I craved, realizing I had not yet begun my new life.

After two weeks in L.A., I devised a plan. I would go back disguised as a different person. I haunted the used clothing stores on Melrose, and purchased a black, ankle length skirt with a slit up the side and high black boots. I found a large, scuffed man's leather jacket and a stylish black beret that I wore off to the side, reminding me of my sister Deborah. I colored my hair black and, by the end of the third week, the redhead in a white turtleneck and jeans was no more. I returned to Prince and Bowery, stepping out of the cab at midnight onto the silent, empty, icy street. Quickly, I dashed up to my apartment, refraining from turning on lights. The street lamp on the corner shined into the large open space, creating a muted soft light. I lit a candle in the bathroom to brush my teeth and climbed into bed.

The next morning, I called the Chinese hardware on Lispenard, instead of the close-by Mafia-run store on Bowery, to measure for window shades throughout the apartment. I kept the shades down, letting in filtered light during the days that followed, and at night I installed dim lights. No one knew I was there.

I stayed away from Ray's and walked in and out of the apartment in my crazy black garb, wearing large sunglasses, never answering the doorbell. When it rang, I looked down through a slit in the shades, and saw Tony Desario looking up at my window, wondering if he was really attracted to me, or if his Mafia family had hired him to watch me. He always walked left, going west on Prince toward Gotti's clubhouse or the Old Saint Patrick's Church they all attended.

I sat in that apartment with the shades down. That glorious room which had made me dance and sing with the glistening light during the day, and sparkled from cars at night, now was closed from the world. I could not pick up a brush. The new aluminum cart with my paints spread out so neatly next to a palette and brushes in the coffee can sat there waiting to be used. I asked myself: *Why am I here? I gave up my home, good friends and family to come to this shaded fishbowl and sit here, mute. God, what have I done?*

I put on my disguise and took the elevator down, running at a mad pace on Bowery and around the corner to Spring Street and the galleries. Each one I surveyed confirmed my being. I was there on a mission; I must never lose sight of that goal: to produce the best work I was capable of and to say something unique, be a revolutionary. It was not the shaded windows that kept me from working, but a lack of inspiration. I had nothing to say. I did not even know who I was any more. I had to reinvent myself.

CHAPTER

15

She Painted the Daffodils

In search of motivation, I took the subway uptown to 57th Street. The Marlborough Gallery was showing German artist Anselm Kiefer's Holocaust Series. I wandered through the exhibition in awe, scrutinizing each gigantic canvas, some with detritus embedded into thick pigment. I surveyed the crowd. The well-known artists, members of the Gallery's stable, were mixed with the struggling, impoverished artists following their dream. I saw few collectors. They had been invited to private showings days before to get first dibs. Kiefer's work sold well.

As the crowd, garbed in black, milled around the packed gallery, I spotted a petite beauty with dark wavy hair and large brown eyes, wearing an oversized puffy scarlet down parka. We were both magnetized by Kiefer's gigantic flaming landscapes and stood side by side for several minutes, sharing our thoughts about the work superficially, as strangers do. We walked to the next canvas and continued chatting. As we came back to the entrance, we agreed to stroll down the block to another reception at the Pace Gallery.

Her name was Suzanne Shapiro, also a painter, but not a part of the downtown art scene. A New Yorker from Brooklyn, she was single, had had a brief marriage with no children, and worked part-time for an advertising agency. We connected on many levels and planned to meet again for openings.

The following Saturday afternoon, we traipsed through the galleries in SoHo, then, exhausted, collapsed at Antonio's in Little Italy for pasta and to expound on the work we had seen. We were quite the duo: I, the redhead in black and she, the brunette in red. Suzanne was not interested in finding a dealer or making a unique statement with her art; she simply loved to paint what she saw, and in those early days in New York, she became my only real friend in the city.

One night after the openings, we were sitting in her tiny, cluttered apartment on East 60th Street above Serendipity, the ice cream parlor. Every inch of her place was filled with small paintings and pigments, bottles of mixes and canvases.

"He called last night and wants to rent in Fire Island for the two of us again this summer," she said.

"What's wrong with that? Sounds like fun."

"I've only heard from him a couple of times all winter; I'm not sure I want to let myself be vulnerable. After my divorce, I bought into a singles' share. I was lonely and wanted new people in my life. I met Ben. Each time I went that first summer, we were together, walking the beach and talking about our lives; didn't even make love."

"Sounds like the beginning of a meaningful relationship."

"After summer ended, I hardly heard from him until the following spring."

Suzanne told me he finally called, wanting to rent a place for just the two of them, from Memorial Day to Labor Day. She was angry about his not calling all winter, and not sure she wanted to go. Her place in the city was so small; she was dying to get out of town by the summer, so she agreed. Of course, they became lovers, had a wonderful time, and then, in the fall, the same thing happened again. She only heard from him occasionally, some winters not at all.

"Was he married? Where'd he live?" I said.

"On the West Side. No, he wasn't married, just shy."

"Why didn't you call him?"

"Guess I'm old-fashioned; I wanted to be pursued and didn't want to seem too eager. I loved going to Fire Island, sitting on the beach, cooking in a real kitchen and being with Ben at night."

She told me that each spring she was so angry with him but relented. She had not met anyone else and asked if I would come this year. She wanted me to meet him; just not sure she was in love.

We decided on the third weekend after Memorial Day and met at Penn Station, waiting for the Long Island Railroad. Ben was a stocky 5′ 8″ guy with dark hair, a prominent nose and chin. He wore jeans and a white T-shirt under a blue blazer, looking clean and stylish. We took the train to Bay Shore, then Tommy's Taxi to the Ferry, which took us out to Ocean Beach. We wore sunglasses and straw hats and sat on the top deck of the ferry in the blazing sun. It was magical as we skimmed the open waters of the Great South Bay. Suzanne was excited about cooking and talked about the menus she was planning. With no cars on the island, Ben pulled the wooden wagon, carrying our suitcases and groceries, while holding onto Suzanne with his other hand.

The house they rented was a simple clapboard with two bedrooms, a living room and a real kitchen; quite a change from the hotplate and toaster oven in her city kitchen. The furnishings at the beach were aged wicker, upholstered in cadmium cotton; a cozy hideaway. Suzanne was a different person away from the city; more vital, like a child celebrating her birthday, racing around, singing while she put groceries away, and then collapsing in the yellow couch. Cooking in a real kitchen was her gift.

Wanting to leave them alone, I gravitated down the long straight path to the water's edge. It was my first time at the Atlantic, and I was surprised to see that the color was green, not the azure blue of the Pacific. Roaming the beach, I picked up dead sea urchins and shells and took a long run. At the end of the day, I laid my treasures out to dry on the deck and vowed to use them in my new series of paintings.

After Labor Day, we resumed our weekend jaunts to the galleries. I noticed Suzanne's enthusiasm waning. She could hardly get through the afternoon.

"What's going on? It looks like you've lost weight. You all right?"

"I'm so tired, always cold, have a little pain in my belly."

"Maybe it's time for a check-up. Think you're pregnant?" I asked.

"I'm terrified to go; my father died so young and I've never felt very fit."

I encouraged her to go in immediately, and I called when she got home from the doctor.

"He wants me to come back for more tests."

"When?"

"Tomorrow."

I took her to New York Hospital by cab, even though it was close to her apartment. We had no idea how long she would be there but thought she would be safe, and whatever was going on would be taken care of. Three days later, I picked her up and we came directly to my apartment. I fed her chicken soup, and she slept on my couch for several days while waiting for the doctor to call.

Her pain intensified. I called her doctor repeatedly and finally he returned our call with the news. She had ovarian cancer, stage four, too advanced for chemotherapy. She went home to get her things together, and to tell Ben and her mother. Two weeks later, she checked into the hospital. The room was a light gray aqua, and she was alone. It was early spring, and I brought daffodils. Ben brought a sketchbook and watercolors. She painted the daffodils and every new flower we brought as she lingered in the hospital room. I went to visit almost every day, and finally asked if there were other people she wanted to see.

"The great love of my life was a guy I met in college, Freddy Eversley. He's a sculptor in L.A. My mom forbade me to see him because he was black. I haven't seen him in years. Could you call him?"

"The world is a small family." I smiled. "I know Fred very well; he's a good friend of mine, and makes luminous, plastic abstractions. He lives and works in a storefront across from my studio in Venice, California." I could understand Suzanne falling in love with him.

Fred was surprised to hear from me out of context, and devastated to learn about Suzanne. He arrived two days later. Tall, thin Fred was a fair-skinned African American, with freckles and an infectious smile, a real character in the Venice art community. To keep Suzanne's mother away while Fred visited, I invited her to lunch, and we shopped for a bathrobe at Bloomingdale's for Suzanne. She kept saying, "Got to get to the hospital. I can't let the day go by without seeing Suzanne." I had a hard time inventing reasons to keep her away.

When Fred left town, and we were alone, Suzanne confessed, "Seeing Freddy after all these years helped me to realize that I really do love Ben. He's been by my side every day. I don't know how, but I'd like to marry him before I die."

I lay down next to her and we sobbed long, deep sobs. I had only known Suzanne two years, but we had become as close as sisters. Time was short. That night I called Ben, worried about what his response would be, not wanting him to feel pressured.

"How would you feel about marrying Suzanne? Would that be something you would want to do?"

"Oh yes! I've loved Suzanne since the day we met. I wasn't sure she would want to marry me; I never really knew how she felt." I realized both had been afraid of rejection all those years.

"You ask her, and I'll arrange the rest," I said. That night when he got home from the hospital, he called.

"I can't believe it; she accepted. I'm so excited."

The following week, with Suzanne's mother, her brother, sister-in-law and I as witnesses in her hospital room, standing next to the rolling cart with the morphine drip, she wore the new white robe her mother had bought on our shopping trip and a veil provided by the hospital. Trembling, she held one red rose while the in-house chaplain married them, with little aplomb. The hospital served apple juice, and her brother brought champagne. Ben stayed with her all that night and held her.

Suzanne died the following week; she was forty-nine.

CHAPTER

16

Mercer Street Studio

After the painful death of Suzanne, my only close friend in Manhattan, I was feeling totally alone in the vast morass of New York City. The openings and frivolity of the galleries had lost their seduction, so I stayed away.

The Mafia boys were at mass in the Old Saint Patrick's Church on Mulberry Street. It was 1989, ten o'clock on a rainy Sunday morning. A year at the Prince Street apartment had passed, and I was glad not to renew my lease. I had met Amy Ernst, the granddaughter of German artist Max Ernst. She wanted to sublet her apartment on East 53rd Street, and I took it while I was deciding where to finally land. The movers and I once again worked tirelessly, packing and piling my belongings into a van. When all was loaded, I casually walked west, past the church, wearing my disguise, and called out to the wind. "Bye, boys, see you around."

Then, at Lafayette Street, I ran down the stairs into the uptown subway. The truck was pulling up as I arrived at East 53rd. We unloaded the furniture and boxes into Amy's small, furnished flat, stuffing it wall to wall. In that claustrophobic space piled high with both our belongings, I felt safe at last.

The Women's Caucus painters group met in each others' studios once a month. The first meeting I attended was in a large, well-lit loft on the Upper West side, with pink bulbs shining onto five 44″ square abstract expressionist canvases in bold, hot colors. Six women sat on card table chairs sipping wine and eating cashews as we commented on the work. I silently prayed they would not appoint me to host the next studio visit. I sensed I was an impostor, having nothing to show, not even one painting. I had not picked up a brush since moving to New York.

In the jumble of Amy's small space, I cleared the dining table to eat and watch her TV. While eating breakfast the following week, a news flash came on: "A tremendous spill of 11.1 million gallons of oil from the Exxon Valdez tanker has run aground on Prince William Sound, Alaska." It smothered the forested shores and sea life. Otters, whales and dolphins were stuck in the oil. Gripped by the disaster, I ran out, bought all the newspapers, and spread the photos out on the table.

As I climbed over chairs and sofas in that tiny space, squeezed between boxes and kitchen supplies, a surge of passion returned. I made sketches from the photos. At last, I had something meaningful to paint about. Eager to experiment with acrylic paints, I took the subway down to Pearl Paint on Canal Street and brought back fresh tubes of pigment, canvases, and nylon brushes.

I started searching *The Village Voice* classifieds, determined to find a real studio to work in. On Mercer Street in SoHo, I went to see a semi-basement, entering at street level, going down six steps into a large white art studio with a twelve-foot ceiling and Corinthian columns. It had an odor of oil paint and turpentine and faced the street, with three large windows high up, and protective bars on the outside. There was a small toilet room and a connecting area with sink and counter for a hot plate, with space underneath for a short refrigerator. My first impression was to dismiss it. *A basement for an art studio? How could I?* But as I saw what else was available, and the high prices of equal spaces in SoHo, I came back. Within a week I was moved in.

During this period, my mother visited me from Los Angeles, and after she left, my children came. We all slept in Amy's small, crowded apartment, but loved the new studio. Overlooking all the negatives, I knew I would at last be actualizing my dream of painting in New York City.

Several months after Mother had gone back to Los Angeles, she called to tell me she was on her way to the hospital. She had gone to aerobics at 8:00 a.m., then her museum class at 10:00, where she started to have chest pains. She could hardly breathe, so she went to see her internist, who drove her directly to Cedars-Sinai Hospital. Mother had needed an angioplasty and called me when she was lucid to tell me she was fine but still in intensive care. The next morning, as they were transferring her to a room, she had a coronary and died. It was so sudden; I was in shock and could not believe how fast she went.

Lena Brown Marinoff had been raised on a sheep and chicken farm in Clarion, Utah until age thirteen, when her family moved to Los Angeles. She had an insatiable thirst for knowledge, was a fine sculptor and writer, and only 76. My brilliant and loving father, George, had died ten years earlier, also from heart problems. I was at once an orphan.

By the time of my mother's death, Amy was eager to move back into her apartment. So, within a day, I had movers again, and all my possessions deposited into my Mercer Street art studio before flying to Los Angeles to settle Mother's affairs.

Three months later, I flew back into Kennedy at dusk. By the time I arrived in SoHo, businesses and galleries were closed and it was nearing midnight. Mercer Street, the alley behind Broadway, gave off an aura of somber gloom. I unlocked the outer street-level door and walked down the stairs to the inner door of my studio. No one lived in the basement. It was ominously silent. I scooted back up the stairs to find an all night deli and grab some food. At that time, SoHo was frighteningly quiet and dark at night. I walked in the middle of the street for fear of being attacked from the shadows of doorways. Back in the studio, I faced my small environmental paintings of the oil spill. They seemed even darker, having just returned from the bright sunshine of Los Angeles.

I lived in the studio for nine months, showering at a gym I had joined in midtown. After living on the frightening Bowery and then squeezed into Amy's small apartment, followed by the studio with no kitchen or shower, I ate dinner with Cherie Stawasz one evening, a New Yorker in advertising who had bought one of my Erotic paintings while in L.A.

"Where would you live, if you had your choice of anywhere in Manhattan?" I asked. She knew how I loved the ocean, and took me to River Court, a tall, red tile building on East 52nd Street between First and the East River. We brazenly took the elevator up to the roof garden as if we owned it, and I feasted on a full view of the river. The lights of the bridges and reflections of the Manhattan skyline seduced me. It was not the ocean, but it was water, and glorious. I went back and rented an apartment on the top, 37th floor, rationalizing that heaven would be the perfect place to live.

I was a jock in those days and bought a white bike. In my helmet and sunglasses, I cycled to my SoHo studio down Second Avenue most days, stopping in Union Square Park for coffee and to watch the chess players and listen to the bongo drums, barking dogs, and singing birds. At the end of the day, I rode back up First Avenue, sometimes taking the subway. The bike ride exhilarated me. However, on some nights, the adrenaline turned to terror when cars honked me off the road and pedestrians gave me the finger. After several years, I limited my bike riding to Central Park on Sundays.

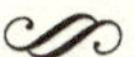

In London several years earlier, I had gone to Saatchi's museum to see the Anselm Kiefer exhibition. Later, at the Marlborough show, Kiefer opened my eyes to experimentation with a greater variety of acrylic mediums. I ordered twelve-foot-wide bolts of heavy canvas and stapled them directly onto my new studio walls. Researching gels and molding paste, I mixed marble dust with pigments to create a thickened texture. When I wandered the streets of SoHo and the sands of Rockaway Beach, I searched for detritus to incorporate into my new work.

I meditated daily, realizing I had come so far to be in New York, but now I faced the hardest challenge: to produce meaningful, original works of art. When the white canvas intimidated me, I threw paint on it, starting with thin washes, letting it dry then going back into it again. As the painting got farther along and an image emerged, I used a palette knife. Stroke by stroke, it became thicker with each application. Focused on producing the new series, I came early each day and often walked out of the studio at 10:00 p.m. dazed, realizing I had forgotten to eat. The days, weeks and months flew by. I was obsessed.

A superb group of eight bright and talented artists invited me to join their morning group, The Manhattan Breakfast Club. We met at Violet's Cafe at 9:00 a.m. every Wednesday and sat at the big round marble table in the far left corner overlooking Washington Square Park near NYU. Tony DeBlasi, Vincent Mastracco, Vincent Baldissano, Anne Elliott, Debra Chase, Helmut Aman, Charles Meyers, Irene Christensen, and I became a family. We talked about who was showing at which gallery, and what was up with the Whitney, MOMA and the Guggenheim. En masse, the whole group walked to my studio to see my work. We were supportive of one another in all respects, held each other's hands through surgeries and illness, and always attended each other's exhibitions.

On Friday nights all winter, through good weather and inclement, at a nearby gallery in SoHo, I met with a group for discussions called "Artists Talk on Art." I became a Board member, and planned panels with art critics, dealers and museum curators discussing all aspects of the creative process and art business. A frenzy of information was constantly being fed to us. I was a sponge, soaking it all up. Planning the panels was a challenge, but I met the art critics Donald Kuspit and Arthur Danto, who became my friends.

On a Wednesday morning, I was in a rush to get from my midtown apartment to the breakfast group, leaving just enough time to ride my bike down Second Avenue to Washington Square Park. I waited for the elevator, standing alone on the top floor pressing the button. Mr. Tremble, from apartment 37C, came with his briefcase, stiffly joining me in his blue suit. Then the nanny from down the hall with her six-year-old twins on their way to school came. The gray-haired woman from 37F with her matching poodle arrived. We all waited . . . ten, fifteen more minutes. Mr. Tremble went back into his apartment and called the front desk.

"The guy downstairs says both elevators are out, systems failure."

"What'll we do?" cried the nanny.

"I'm walking down," I said, as I put my bike back into the apartment.

Mr. Tremble came with me, down the 37 flights. The others decided to stay upstairs. By the time I got to Violet's, everyone had gone. When I returned late that night, the elevator was still out. It was August and hot.

"Electricity's out on the whole Upper East Side," said the guy at the front desk. "Too many air conditioners. Here's a flashlight for the stairs."

With flashlight in hand, I started my ascent up the scary black stairwell, stopping at every second floor to rest, telling myself how good it was for my hips. When I got up to the 37th floor, I felt my way along the darkened hall and four doors over to my apartment. I had no lights, no air, no TV, phone or stove. Thankfully, I had candles.

The next day, the power was still off. Marooned on the top floor, peering out at the East River, the bridges and the skyline, I realized that living in heaven could also be a kind of hell.

I arrived back at my studio that morning out of breath, and noticed the bars over my windows had been crowbarred open. I had been burglarized. I wandered through the studio and noticed missing cameras, an answering machine; small things they could carry. I immediately installed new bars and window shades again, lowering them at night. I slathered my new white bike with ugly brown acrylic paint and became more conservative in my dress, especially on the subway. I learned not to tempt the thieves. This was a different New York than I ever imagined when I was a naive tourist.

I realized I had been a vagabond long enough, and it was time to get one safe place to work and live under the same roof and settle down. I was staying. New York was where I belonged.

CHAPTER

17

Dark Work

It was nearing Thanksgiving. Heavy winds had battered the city and the leaves had fallen. The winter cold had commenced, but inside the well-lit studio with its Corinthian columns and high ceilings, I felt warmth, surrounded by my classical and jazz tapes and with my simmering tea kettle. Finally, I was being productive. After months of hibernation, in spite of the cold, I had the urge to spring loose. In my old ski jacket, hat, gloves and scarf, I dashed over to the river at Canal Street, jogged down to the Battery, then back up, the icy cold stinging my face. I was alive. The run cleared my head and made me eager to get back to work. Running late in the day became my ritual. Taking different routes each time, I explored the grisly side streets of Little Italy, Chinatown, and the Financial District. Then I ran over to the river and back up to my studio, maneuvering the cobblestones and dodging loading docks.

The following week on my run, I passed a foreclosure sign on a loft building on Franklin Street in Tribeca, drawing me back into the web of real estate. I immediately called the broker listed on the sign and, before I knew it, I was looking at a vast, 3200-square-foot first floor with seventeen-foot ceilings, slammed up against the back and side of buildings, light emanating only from the front windows. I walked from one end to the other, thinking: *the price is so low I could actually afford this.* I needed to show it to someone who could help me make a decision. The broker recommended an architect named Don Weston. Don, a few years older than I, was slight, with warm, convivial eyes, graying brown hair, and arrived two days later wearing brown tweed and carrying a leather briefcase. We wandered through the loft together.

"The deal is just too good to pass up," he said. "If you don't buy it, I will."

I agreed on the price with the foreclosing bank and thought the sale final, but soon found that buying distressed property in New York City was fraught with litigation. I subsequently attended fifteen court hearings. After explaining my plight to my old Mafia friend from the Prince and Bowery neighborhood, he escorted me to a hearing. After sitting through the rhetoric at the lower Manhattan courthouse, he said, "Want me to put a contract out on her?"

Frightened, I backed off, deciding it was not worth the fight. The bank made me sign papers, agreeing not to publicize that they had sold me unavailable property, and they paid my moving and storage costs. I stayed in my Mercer Street studio, rented a temporary apartment, and continued commuting. The owner of the loft, a 40-year-old Chinese woman who had been housing boat people who worked in the garment factories, sleeping in the makeshift, dormitory-style second floor, won her case.

My friendship with Don Weston remained strong. We spoke the same language, sharing our love of structural design and renovation. When he was in my neighborhood, he would drop in to see my newest paintings, and we would go around the corner to Manhattan Bistro for lunch.

By mid May, after isolating myself in the studio the whole winter, I opened the windows and, as if by magic, nature had painted the tree blossoms pink and white overnight. I confessed to Don that coming to New York late in life, I found it hard to meet established artists, especially single men.

"There's someone I know you will enjoy meeting," he said, and told me about a client of his, a Greek named Nassos Daphnis, who showed with Leo Castelli's gallery.

"You have a lot in common, and he's single."

The following week, late in the day when SoHo was quiet, we arrived at Nassos's studio, a dark gray landmark building on the corner of West Broadway and Broome. As we waited for him to answer the black steel door, I thought about the contrast to my former life of tree lined, ocean view avenues in Pacific Palisades, California.

Nassos greeted us with a wide grin and flashing eyes, ushering us into his first floor, crumbling loft. He was twenty years my senior, a short man in paint-strewn khakis, with a warmth that lit up the darkening sky. I looked around in awe. The peeling tin ceiling was sixteen feet high. He had built a sleeping loft above the simple kitchen and the rest of the space was all art studio. Every inch of the massive space was filled with his hard-edged geometrical paintings in primary colors. He made up for his diminutive size by working large. The odor of oil-based house paint was intense, and his mixing surface was a large dining table. The only wall not covered with paintings was his working wall. In the rear, were floor-to-ceiling racks filled with 50 to 60 canvases. I thought: *this guy's real. Finally, I'm in the presence of serious work.*

When Nassos was in the kitchen rustling up drinks, I asked Don, "How do you know him?"

He shielded his mouth with one hand and whispered, "I did some work for him a few years ago. . . . He still hasn't paid me." He told me that when Nassos sells a painting, and he gets big bucks, he invests in another building. Never had cash, typical of artists who had been there since the sixties when property was cheap. Nassos came back in, removed a pile of magazines and sketches from the table and gave us each a glass of white wine, motioning to sit up on the high stools in front of his new canvas.

The following week Nassos invited me to dinner. I brought a bottle of Pinot Grigio and, in his little kitchen, set with flickering candles, he served me lightly broiled salmon smothered in a delicate cream sauce, wild rice and a tomato salad. Meeting Nassos was a rare gift. He became my benevolent friend and mentor. I treasured his kind spirit and innate wisdom.

We scooted from gallery to gallery in SoHo on Saturdays, wanting to see all the shows at Paula Cooper, Mary Boone, Nancy Hoffman and Ileana Sonnabend's galleries. We always ended up on the fourth floor at 420 West Broadway, Leo Castelli's gallery. After each opening, Leo would have a private reception for his artists in a restaurant, honoring the painter or sculptor being shown. I felt honored to be included, but secretly aspired to also be a member of that stable. Some evenings, when we were not invited to a dinner or reception after trudging through the shows, we would veer from the path to Zarre's gallery at closing and schmooze with Andre. It was a grand space with high ceilings and well lit. Nassos had shown with him in the past and they'd become close friends. Andre was an eccentric, corpulent man with a round face and thinning gray-blond hair; some called him "The Buddha." Visiting became our ritual. Andre would turn the lights off except for the spots over his reception area and sit with legs stretched out straight, crossed over one another on the counter and we would draw up chairs facing him.

"Got any new gossip for us, Andre?" Nassos asked.

"You see the Whitney Biennial yet? The work stinks. Can't believe they hung that junk."

He was always ready with an unexpected comment. We laughed it off, but knew Andre strived for quality, was astute, and we realized he must have been insulted by what he saw. The Biennial was always *the show critics loved to hate.*

Day after day, I raced downtown by bike from midtown, then ran down the stairs into my studio and heated water on my hot plate for jasmine tea. I sat in front of my latest canvas with a brush or sometimes a palette knife in hand and went to work. Nassos often knocked on my window and I'd buzz him in. He'd go directly to the little black couch and, in his old painting clothes, drinking tea as I painted, he'd command me:

"You've got to work harder, paint larger, produce more," as he watched me laboriously apply layer upon layer of pigment, mixed with gels and marble dust.

As we drank our tea, we questioned our obsession with making art.

"We've been appointed by a higher power to leave our mark on the world." Nassos stressed that future generations would understand our history more astutely through our markings. We were two souls lost to our art.

Other artists down the long hallway had to pass my studio as they entered and left the building. When my door was open, some would wander in. Often, art dealers would come in. One day, three dealers tapped on my open door.

One was rather heavy with a beard and motorcycle sunglasses, in jeans and a New York Knicks hat; the other two were well-groomed, in suits and ties. They introduced themselves, shaking my hand.

"Feel free to look around," I said, as they walked to each canvas, pulling out two from the racks while chatting among themselves. The tall, lean one in a black suit nudged the other dressed-up fellow.

"Your work's too dark; I don't think we can sell it, but thanks anyway." They wrote my name and phone number in their small leather book and walked out.

After they left, I sat down to catch my breath, incensed. I grabbed a cup of tea and a cookie, then went to the rolling cart and mixed ultramarine deep, and raw umber, slathering it on to make the paintings even darker. Yes, they were dark. No one was going to tell me what colors to paint. SoHo was dark, Mercer Street was the bleak alley behind Broadway, my subject was the devastation of our environment inspired by the oil spill, and I was in a dark mood. It was essential that the work be dark.

After almost six years, I was at a turning point and believed it was crucial that my work be shown. Yet the realization that nothing would happen unless I asserted myself had a numbing effect. Sending slides and buttering up art dealers went against my nature. I had had successful exhibitions in Los Angeles, Denver, and Frankfurt, mostly from showing my Erotic and Synergistic series, but was immobilized by fear in New York's more competitive atmosphere. I shared my quandary with Nassos, who had been with Castelli for 25 years and could not relate. He decided to bring Andre Zarre over to get his take on the work. Andre said he would come if Nassos brought him, making it clear that he would not commit himself if he had any reservations about the work.

It was a Tuesday night around eight. They had been out for dinner, and Nassos called to tell me they were on their way.

"I'm here, give me fifteen," I said as I nervously placed the work around the studio. Most of the paintings were 8′ x 10′, heavy to lift with the many layers of pigment, some on unstretched canvas stapled to the walls, about twenty all together. I had three standing photoflood lamps with blue bulbs to bring out the color.

Nassos tapped on the window and I buzzed them in. They came down the stairs, then into the studio.

Wearing my old paint-spattered lab coat, I welcomed them with cheek kisses. Nassos and I walked with Andre to the center of each work, explaining the premise of the series.

I held my breath as Andre studied each painting; glad my Erotic series was safely hidden in my Venice studio so he would not be distracted. On the outside I was calm and quiet, but on the inside my stomach churned. For six years, I had been looking forward to exhibiting work in New York that would give me some quantity of regard in the art community. It hinged on this moment. In the final analysis, respect was all I yearned for.

After a long silence, while searching into each work, Nassos and Andre sat down on the black couch. I offered them sherry. Andre sipped it slowly, not saying a word, his left leg bobbing up and down. Nassos winked at me. I blinked both eyes in response. With a serious tone that I could not read, Andre looked at me and said, "They're really very good, Elaine. I would be honored to show them. How about September, the first exhibition after the summer's lull?"

I breathed at last. "A perfect time," I said.

Andre had an embarrassingly hard time getting out of the low sofa. Nassos pulled him up. I wanted to help but turned away, knowing how sensitive he was about his weight.

As I heard them walk up the stairs and the door slam shut, I jumped up and down and said, "Yay!" clapping my hands like a five-year-old. It wasn't Castelli, but it was a reputable dealer with a fine gallery, who had an honest respect for the work. What more could I ask for at this stage? I gave myself the gift of a taxi ride home.

The Friday after Andre and Nassos had been at the studio, at an Artists Talk on Art weekly discussion group, Robert C.

Morgan, an art historian and critic, spoke about his new book, *After the Deluge: Essays for Art in the Nineties.* Fascinated, I bought the book. After reading it, I called on a hunch and invited him to make a studio visit. He remembered me and said he would be delighted.

A week later, Morgan came to the studio, tall and thin, his face ruddy and radiant, wearing jeans and a brown herringbone blazer with leather elbow patches. His confident aura enveloped my being. I was still in a state of childlike excitement from the week before, babbling on enthusiastically, the antithesis to my reserve with Andre. I asked him, without thinking, if he would write an essay for a catalog I planned to put together for my exhibition.

"Not sure," he said. "Need to examine the work first."

I switched on the photofloods and stepped over to my desk, pretending to read some paperwork. I was again at someone's mercy, this time the art critic. He was such a fox. As he perused the paintings, I fantasized: *sure wish I were ten years younger. I'll bet he's great in bed. It's been so long.*

Robert Morgan spent half an hour inspecting the paintings, then came over and said, "How about that tea you offered? Got any cookies?" I found some oatmeal raisin in the cabinet, pulled up a chair and we sat by my desk, munching. He looked at me and said, "It would be my pleasure to write the essay for your catalog."

After he left, I realized he gave no hint of his response to the work. Did he even understand what it was about? I had acted so spontaneously that I felt foolish. I realized that an important art critic had just consented to write an essay on my work. I had to trust him, but what he might say terrified me.

I waited patiently for a month, and then let him know I was going to Los Angeles to put together the catalog. He had the manuscript delivered just as I was headed to the airport. I read it on the plane.

He called the series: "Marinoff's Inner Nature." A partial quote from Robert C. Morgan's essay:

Elaine Marinoff is an intuitive painter. Her references are both external (nature) and internal (metaphysical). One might speak of her paintings as a dialectical search of an equivocation between what she perceives as happening in nature and the balance she attempts to strike within herself . . . as someone capable of transforming what she sees into a cataclysmic sense of reality. Yet this cataclysm also has a certain harmonious aspect, a redemptive side. Her paintings are visibly dark. . . . One may look for crevices, and openings. There is a certain tension on the surfaces of her paintings that is more spatial than formal. This distinction is a necessary one in order to come to terms with Marinoff's working method. Marinoff states that she is interested in "the delicate balance of our complex ecosystem at this time in history." Her paintings are thick, dense and eroded in their appearances, as if to suggest the pollution of the earth is woven into the fabric of our rivers and waterways . . .

I reread it two more times. *I think he liked them.* Euphoric, my ear-to-ear grin lit up the entire coach section of the Boeing 747.

CHAPTER

18

The Packed Gallery Buzzed

September 8, 1994, was my opening night. SoHo was still the center of New York's art scene. On the ground floor of the Andre Zarre gallery at 48 Greene, with windows facing the street, a large crowd garbed in black could be seen standing in groups. Cars lined up around the block, limo drivers waiting. The gallery consisted of two large open spaces, fourteen-foot ceilings and polished cement floors. My new dark, acrylic environmental paintings were sparsely hung on the white walls. The *New Yorker's* listing, *Art In America's* full-page spread, and Robert C. Morgan's essay in the catalog proclaimed the work's creative value. The packed gallery buzzed and corks popped. In a black suit and high heels, I boldly received collectors and friends with an ear to ear, frozen grin, my right hand weak by the end of the reception. I was thrilled and surprised to see my daughter, Cindy, and her husband, here from Atlanta, and other out of town friends showing up. Like a love affair finally come to fruition, the exhibition was the grand crescendo.

After three intense hours of greeting guests, my dear mentor, Nassos, eyes crinkled with age, garbed in brown, his gray hair slicked back, glanced at his watch and gently grabbed my elbow. "We should leave, it's eight o'clock."

"But they're all still here."

"Come on, the invitation says it ends at eight. It's enough. Let Andre deal with the rest."

Nassos and I discreetly migrated to Mercer Street in the dim light of early evening, then descended the stairs into my basement studio. I collapsed on the black couch while he set out the wine glasses.

One after the other, twenty close friends, mostly artists in their forties and fifties from the breakfast group, wandered in after being checked off by the art student with my list at the door. The pork fried rice, almond chicken, and green beans from Ming Cho on Mott Street arrived. We placed the platters on a lace cloth covering my paint-mixing table, pushing brushes, tubes of paint and gels to the side. The crowd stood, sat on stools, or squeezed into the little black couch, rehashing the show. I heard Debra say, "I saw Sam Oblenski from *ARTNews* run through the show, then duck out."

"Same with Ivan Karp," Charles said. "Before I could grab him, he was a block away."

They all agreed my first New York show was a success, as they drank the cheap wine and maneuvered chopsticks, typical of what the art crowd in the city did after openings.

By the time the last guest walked out the door, slightly drunk and alone at last, I was grateful to Nassos and Andre who made it happen, and to the collectors who considered my work valuable enough to purchase. Turning the lights off, I sat in my darkened studio, with the glow of one white candle, remembering all those long, lonely nights in my marriage, waiting for Bob, who called my passion for painting childish. I was proud that I had made my dream into a reality, but panic mixed with gratitude shot through me. *I did it this time; will I be able to do it again?*

CHAPTER

19

The Cliff as Metaphor

After the exhibition reception, I stayed away from the studio for weeks, sequestering myself mostly in Andre's gallery, explaining the work to all who came. I wandered in and out of every gallery in SoHo, assessing the work. Friends came to see my show and I took them to my two haunts: e Street Bar or the Manhattan Bistro. When the exhibition came down, paintings sold were delivered, unsold work was sent back to my studio, and I was paralyzed. Confronted with a profound emptiness, I realized I had to start all over.

As a distraction once again, I went on the hunt for real estate, my comfort zone. Expanding my search to the commercial section of *The New York Times,* I located a first floor and basement, a packaging factory, in the same area as the previous loft on Franklin Street, in Tribeca. I was seduced by the massiveness of the space and knew immediately it was right. That very day, I went to lunch with the broker to discuss it, and the same night, called him with an offer. I secured a mortgage and planned a total gut renovation. It was an all-artists' co-op and they were disparagingly difficult, but I persevered. The loft had two sides with arches dividing it. A 2,500-square-foot studio on one side, and a 2,500square-foot apartment on the other, with 3,000 feet in the windowed basement for storage.

My son Glendon used to say, "Mom, if you spent as much time marketing your art as you do on your real estate deals, you would be way ahead in your art career."

"You're right," I said, "but building and renovating is creative, and it gives me a sense of power, the antithesis to the fine art world, and it allows me to paint without needing to satisfy dealers."

On a hot July afternoon, I was sitting at my drafting table in the Mercer Street studio, working on plans for the new loft, when my former husband Bob called. Hearing his familiar voice was like talking to a long-lost brother. I suddenly felt closer to him than during most of our 21-year marriage.

"What's going on? Still in love with New York?" he asked.

"Sure am, even more so now. I'm painting again. My new work talks about environmental issues. I just had a show," I said. "What about you?"

He told me he had decided to retire and move to Hamilton, Montana, and go fishing.

"I've been thinking," Bob said. "Would you like to come?"

There was a long silence.

"What are you saying? Are you serious?"

"Yes, you could paint, and I'd fish. The kids could come on holidays, and we'd grow old together like we originally planned."

"Oh Bob, I can't leave now; this is where I need to be." I said. "You're only 59. Isn't it too soon to retire?"

"The malpractice insurance is killing me, and I feel lousy; I'm having difficulty breathing."

I realized that all those years of smoking had taken their toll. My feelings of alienation had faded since our divorce. Now I thought of Bob as family. For so many years when we were married,

I prayed we would grow old together, and was touched now by his request. We hung up, and a profound sadness overwhelmed me.

I soon heard from the children that he married his young office manager, Kathy Meeks, and she went with him to Montana. Bob needed a wife.

With the renovation underway, I became increasingly obsessed with my declining finances. Construction always costs more that we anticipate. I wanted desperately to stay in New York and make art but realized that I could not bring in enough cash to live on through the sale of my paintings. I had a paying tenant in my L.A. house perched on the cliff, but was plagued by the fragility of that bluff, and financial survival should that land collapse. Jeopardizing the cliff's security even further, Occidental Petroleum had recently applied for a permit to drill oil under my property.

My contractors at the loft were tearing down walls and putting up new ones. Back in my Mercer Street studio, I decided to lighten up and be more fluid, instead of working in heavy impasto. I ordered a large roll of five-foot wide backdrop paper from Pearl Paint. I climbed to the top of my ten-foot ladder and pulled the paper to the ceiling, stapling it to the wall, then cut it off at the floor, creating a tall, wide surface on which to work. I gathered up old oil pastels, took out my tape deck and slid in a jazz cassette. Instead of a paintbrush this time, I danced, with a drawing stick in hand. The music inspired me, reverberating against the hard surfaces of the studio walls and wood floor. It had been five months since I last put a brush to canvas. The freeing experience of drawing in pastels on paper helped me work with renewed vigor.

When the first roll was used up, I upgraded to a French archival paper. The premise of my new series was the high cliff as my metaphor for the fragility of life, realizing that if my cliff collapsed, so would my life.

I let surprise strokes lead the way. Before I knew it, each drawing took on a life of its own. Entwined lovers and wild animals emerged, intermingling with the elaborate cliffs.

Each day I came again to my dim basement studio at sun-up, through the crowded, noisy streets by bike, climbed up on the ladder to work, then pedaled home after dark.

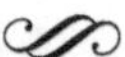

In the new loft, I built two totally separate spaces, one to live in and one for the work. On the left side, I made a packing and crating area near the entrance. Then I left a long narrow art studio empty, with north light filtering in through skylights at the far end, one-third into the room. The long walls with no windows gave me space to work on the drawings. I made a giant glass-topped rolling cart for supplies. The little black couch fit in an alcove with a table and lamp for reading and gave art dealers a comfortable place to sit while viewing the work. My desk and drafting table sat under the skylight.

At last, I moved in. This time the van picked up from both the apartment and art studio, moving everything into one address. I couldn't wait to get up in the morning and step over to my studio and work. Some nights I would wander over at odd hours just to look or pick up a pastel and draw in my pajamas and robe.

Once I was settled, I flew back to my studio in Los Angeles. I unstretched, rolled and boxed eighty paintings and carefully wrapped the remaining portraits, my Synergistic series and the Erotic series of lovers. Then I shipped them to my new studio in New York on Franklin Street and closed my Venice studio for good. When the work arrived, I placed them wrapped in the newly constructed basement storage racks where I knew no one would see them.

They were my secret past.

CHAPTER

20

Joan and the San Andreas Fault

When twenty of the new, immense drawings were completed, I had them photographed and made a presentation to The Drawing Center, a highly respected exhibition space for works on paper. They asked me to bring over the actual works. I rolled up six of my favorites and carried them under my arm from Franklin Street north, crossing Canal, then through the mess of knock-off shops and wandering tourists, stumbling over the cobblestones to Wooster Street. In the rear room of the Alternative space at the Drawing Center, I unrolled each one on a gigantic table. Two young curators scrutinized them.

"We need to get Ann over here," one of the curators said. Ann Philbin, the director, rushed over from the main gallery across the street. They agreed that the drawings were exceptional and wanted to plan an exhibition.

I was elated. Everything I had hoped for was at once coming to fruition.

At 8:00 the next morning, I was exercising in my living room and turned on the news. It was January 17th, 1994.

"At 4:31 a.m. Pacific Standard Time, an earthquake of 6.7 on the Richter scale hit the San Fernando Valley outside Los Angeles and parts of Santa Monica, on the San Andreas Fault line."

Oh my God, I'm on the San Andreas Fault. The valley is so far away; I hope it missed my property.

An hour later the phone rang; it was a friend of my son and daughter, who lived in Venice. After hearing the news, he took a run along the beach to see if there was damage up the coast. He saw that under my property, land had fallen, so much soil that it closed Pacific Coast Highway. He ran up the hill and over to my house.

"Elaine, the earthquake hit your entire street. Some of the houses went down the cliff, but your home is still standing. The upstairs water heater has burst, and water is running throughout the house. The brick fireplaces are all down in piles, and there's glass and debris everywhere. Your tenant must have been terrified and run out, leaving the front door wide open."

I was stunned. My worst fears had been actualized. This was what my drawings were about.

"Close the door, please. I'll get there as soon as possible."

"I don't have the key to lock it up. You'd better get here fast."

On my flight the following day the silent cabin, packed to capacity, gave me the sense that all were en route to Los Angeles for the same reason. Every sullen face seemed distraught, creating an ominous, frightening aura.

I thought about my tenants, Joan and Melissa Rivers, and recalled the day Joan came to look at my house, all prim and proper, after her husband Edgar Rosenberg died and she had sold her Beverly Hills home.

I was in my front yard dressed in shorts and sun hat, my hair in a ponytail, watering my roses. I saw the black limo pull up and park in front of the house. Joan stepped out and, beside her, a hairdresser with brush in hand, who proceeded to smooth down Joan's hair. Immaculately coiffed, she came in alone as if on stage, opening my green-weathered gate, then adjusted her trim black suit, and noticed me. Assuming I was the housekeeper or gardener, she said, "Could you please tell Mrs. Good that I am here?"

"I'm Mrs. Good, come on in."

Taken aback, she wandered in slowly, walking into the living room, then carefully from one room to the next. I sat quietly in the kitchen waiting. She came in at last and said, "I just flew in. Haven't eaten a thing all day. I'm famished. Got any crackers?"

I pulled out a box of Wheat Thins and handed them to her. "Want some cheese to go with them?"

"No, I'm on a diet."

She sat at the kitchen table, eating directly out of the box, staring out the window at the azure Pacific. "I love it," she said. "We'll take it. The ocean soothes my jangled nerves."

Joan and Melissa Rivers stayed in my house five years. They never came back after running out the day of the earthquake.

CHAPTER

21

CBGB's and Hilly

I had only one relative in New York, my cousin Annette, a jazz drummer. She was a great comfort, checking in often. Repeatedly, she asked me to meet a distant cousin, Hilly Kristal, whose grandmother was our grandfather's half-sister in Ukraine.

"You'll really like him; he has a rock and roll club called CBGB's."

"But Annette, rock and roll isn't music to my ears, it's just wild noise. I'm an opera lover."

"Just meet him, he's family. You'll like him and he's anxious to meet you."

After a while, she became exasperated and finally let it go. Months later, an artist friend mentioned a new gallery in town that he thought would be a good place to show his paintings. It was in the CBGB's rock club.

"They're showing outsider art like mine," he said. "Know anything about it?"

"The guy who owns that club is a distant relative. I don't know him, but I'll arrange an introduction for you."

I felt awkward but called Hilly to set up a meeting at my studio. My first vision of him as he walked in was that he was a burly man, at least six feet tall, with a head of wavy gray-brown hair, and a full salt and pepper beard. He wore jeans and a plaid shirt under a fleece vest and seemed quiet and reserved. It was strange introducing him when I had never met him myself, but he greeted me with a big grin and a warm handshake. He looked around my studio at the dark work returned from my exhibition and said, "Finally, we meet. You really are an artist! The paintings are intense, tell me about them."

He seemed genuinely interested, and when he saw my friend's slides, he agreed to show his colorful, figurative paintings in the new gallery. As he left, he bellowed, in his low baritone voice, "I'd love to show you the club, Elaine. It's intense, like your work. Please come by."

After our meeting, I was consumed with my renovation and did not see Hilly for weeks. He called several times to invite me to the club, but I kept making excuses.

I wanted to celebrate when the remodeling was completed. Cousin Annette, her fiancé and I planned a dinner with a girlfriend of mine and her daughter. Annette suggested we invite Hilly. This time I agreed. On the apartment side, pristine white walls and my monumental paintings set off burnt-sienna, leather Le Corbusier sofas. My son Glendon, who designed furniture, made the aluminum base for the thick oval glass dining table. Candles lit up the vast space, and the table sparkled with tall wine glasses and red plates. Hilly came in, beaming, loaded down with wine and an armload of red roses. He hardly spoke all evening. I could not understand how someone who ran a busy, rollicking club night after night would be so reserved. Later, I realized he was just a quiet guy. My girlfriend got him in the corner and talked non-stop. After they left, she said, "Your cousin Hilly is adorable; do you mind if I pursue him?"

"Go ahead," I said. But deep down I was angry with her, and mostly at myself, for not recognizing how special he was.

He called to thank me for the dinner. "Can I ever get you to come to the club?" I realized that I was just afraid to go back over to the Bowery. The wild rock and roll scene was so foreign to me.

The next week he called again, "I have a classical guitarist coming Saturday night. I know you love classical; this time you must come."

The year was 1995. In black jeans and a black leather jacket, I arrived by cab. It was a drizzly May night. Winos were warming their hands above open fires in cylindrical trash cans next to the club's entrance. CBGB's was squeezed between the Amato Opera House and a shelter. A hint of urine floated in the air around the homeless who were hanging out near the club's entrance. Kids wearing chains and spiked green or purple hair, with piercings were waiting in line, a scene forever imprinted upon my mind. I thought of my conservative ex-husband, Bob, always immaculately groomed in his Brooks Brothers suit and tie.

Hilly was there in his black T-shirt with white CBGB letters as the cab pulled up. He helped me out and, taking my arm, guided me ahead of the throngs. The odor of pot wafted through the darkened music hall as a sharp spotlight shined on Joey Ramone, playing guitar and singing on stage at the far end. The gaudy walls, plastered with vintage posters, news clippings, and old photos of sexy Southern belles along with the densely packed crowd, startled my senses.

"Come on, I've got to show you the basement," Hilly said, as his beefy hand grabbed mine. Stepping down the rickety stairs, I felt a warm energy stir through me with his touch.

"Tonight's party down here is to celebrate the opening of this new space. It was raw cement when I started. The people you see are all friends I've invited, not the usual customers." I became conscious of the fact that we were both involved in renovation projects at the same time.

Red, orange, and yellow lights in overhead fixtures and low lamps, created a rosy glow as Hilly's friends sat around on sofas listening to Juicy Lucy and country blues on the sound system. Hilly beamed as he walked me around the room, hand in hand, introducing me to everyone. It was like an enormous family gathering. He wanted me to know that he had built the first floor and basement bars entirely himself, pointing out that he was also creative.

We went next door where he had recently opened an art gallery by the entrance and, in the rear, had poetry readings where a classical guitarist was playing as guests sat by candle-lit tables. We slid side by side into a booth, watching the guitarist while sipping Chablis. The touch of his knee against mine aroused something deep within me. My first instinct was to run away, afraid, after my failed marriage and subsequent broken heart, but I held firm. At the close of the evening, he flagged down a cab, helped me in, and kissed my cheek as he closed the door; I sped away.

Back in my studio, I closed myself off from the world and spoke to almost no one for weeks, except Nassos and Hilly, while drawing my magical, frightening cliffs. I continued to spend Saturdays with Nassos, going to the galleries and dinner. That was Hilly's biggest night at the club. But Hilly's low baritone voice at the beginning and end of each day warmed its way into my heart.

After I had worked eight to ten hours on my drawings alone in my studio, he talked me into hopping a cab and coming to the rollicking club just to sit inconspicuously on the side, and hold his hand, while Patti Smith or Blondie sang. The seediness of the club became familiar, and I started to consider it another art form.

When Hilly could get away, we walked ten minutes from my loft to the Hudson River to watch the sunset over New Jersey. We strolled south along the waterside path from Chambers Street to the blue lights reflected on the river at the end, where we found a small hidden fish restaurant. Walking back, I slipped my arm through his and, while gazing at New Jersey, he told me about being raised on the chicken farm in Hightstown. He had studied violin as a child, then trained to be an opera singer, a baritone. We sat down on an iron bench, and he told me that after several appearances at Radio City Music Hall, he started the first open-air theater in Central Park with Ron Delsener.

"Then I opened a restaurant that served fowl in the Village, where I used Mother's recipes from the farm." He told me after that he went in the direction of new music and worked at the Village Vanguard before opening his own club, Hilly's, on 9th, and then, CBGB's.

"When I set up the club, my one rule was that all my musicians play only what they themselves had composed. I wanted original sounds, new voices." He loved talking about the club, and I was mesmerized by his low voice and life story. The era of punk rock was just emerging, and that great big, bearded hunk, Hilly Kristal, became one of the founding fathers. If he liked a band, he would support it and take them on the road. Helping those young musicians get somewhere in the music industry gave him a sense of purpose. I realized he was ahead of his time in so many ways, in fashion as well as music. I always wondered how he knew what would be next.

We had taken that walk on so many afternoons. Some days we just sat on the iron bench, holding each other's arm and not speaking until the ball of sun disappeared behind New Jersey. We would get up, as if by magic, in unison, and continue walking. When we reached my loft, he would gently kiss my cheek and walk on back to the club. Each time he left me bereft, wanting him more. He was so shy and even though I was feeling stronger in my art career somehow I could not bring myself to be the aggressor. We were both afraid to allow ourselves to be vulnerable.

Then one night as he started to leave, I blurted out, "Want to come in and have a cup of tea?"

"Sure, great idea."

He followed me into the kitchen, and I opened the drawer with my stash of loose tea and boxes of bags. "Pick what you like," I said as I reached up into the cupboard for cups.

"Want honey?"

We wandered into the living room carrying our tea. I flipped on the lamp as he sat in the corner of the brown leather sofa; I perched down at the other end. We must have stayed that way, sipping our tea, for twenty minutes, and then all at once his arm reached over and pulled me close. My head snuggled onto his shoulder for a long while, and I found myself pulling away, trying to tell him that I was frightened, afraid our relationship would never work.

Even though we were from the same original family, we were from two totally different worlds. I had spent months, even years, dreaming of being with him, and I knew he felt the same; but suddenly I was so afraid I would get hurt again.

His head went down into his hands. He got up slowly and, without looking at me or uttering a word, he walked toward the door. I sat transfixed. Then realizing what I had done, went after him as he walked out. I followed him down the darkened Franklin Street, tripping on the curb. The night was chilly. I ran as fast as I could and caught up with him; he shrugged me off. Then he turned around and pulled me close, holding so tight I thought my bones would break. He was so strong.

"Sweetheart," he said, "we've just found each other. Let's give it a chance. We both have difficult pasts. I love you so." His face was cold, but his lips were steaming.

We stood there holding each other on that empty, dark street until we slowly walked back to the loft in silence. He led me into the bedroom. It was the first time, after wanting each other for the two years since we had met.

"We need each other; this is right, I know it," he said hesitantly, as we undressed one another. Naked, we came together trembling. Very gently, he helped me up onto the high bed and we lay holding each other close. He kissed my eyes, then my cheeks, and my mouth at last. I felt the surge of life within me as never before. At first, we made gentle, sweet love, then passionate, then wild love, and stayed entwined until the light of morning. The scent of his body, surprisingly, was the same as mine. The warmth of his large arms and hulky frame made me feel at once comforted and protected. We both had finally found our soul mates. I was 60 and he, 63.

CHAPTER

22

Just Like Hemingway

It was three a.m. several years later. I was snuggled in the bed of my new loft when I heard a faint ringing in the distance. Thinking I was dreaming, I disregarded it and dozed back to sleep. I had turned off the ringer on my bedroom phone years before when friends from California called at all hours, forgetting the time change. It started again, and rang several times until I finally picked up.

"Mom, Dad has died."

Half asleep, I needed time to register what Cindy was saying. "What? When?"

"Just now, Kathy called. His body is still in the driveway; she doesn't know what to do, who to call."

Barely awake, I said, "Tell her to call 911, or the police."

"Thanks, Mom."

I settled back in bed, thinking about Bob. Just two weeks before, I had called to wish him Happy Father's Day. I told him more about my relationship with Hilly and our plans to go to China. Hilly was the only man I had mentioned to Bob since our divorce. He told me his breathing had become worse, and he was in terrible pain. I asked him how he was handling it. "With Scotch and Tylenol, but every breath is a struggle."

Two years before, he'd seen a mass on a simple chest X-ray after a checkup, and flew from Montana to Los Angeles to see John

Benfield, a good friend and thoracic surgeon at the Norris Cancer Center. Bob insisted on scheduling surgery to get the tumor out. He assumed it was lung cancer. The surgeons took out four ribs to get to the tumor, the size of a fist, only to find after a biopsy that it consisted of tuberculosis. He did not need the surgery. It could have been cured with drugs. After years of smoking, he had developed emphysema. His heart was weak, and he'd developed adhesions in his lungs after the surgery. He made trips to a pain clinic, but mostly doctored himself while living in the remote hills of Montana.

We considered suing the hospital, but John Benfield was our close friend. John flew to New York to see me after Bob's death. I said, "John, why didn't you do a biopsy before cutting him open? How could you have been so negligent?"

His ears turned deep red and his hands started shaking. "You know Bob; he demanded we get that goddamn tumor out pronto, insisting we cut immediately."

"But you were the doctor."

"I know, I know, the fact plagues me daily."

I am sure we could have won our case. But at that time, I was no longer married to Bob. The children would have been on their own, fighting in court, and John would have been destroyed. We just did not feel it was worth the battle.

Still in bed, sleep eluded me. Once more I heard a ringing in the distance. This time I picked it up; the clock read 4:30 a.m.

"Mom, Kathy needs your help in writing the obituary."

I thought: *Of course, how could she know the details of Bob's life? She came in when he was already established. I knew him from the beginning.* I put on my robe and walked into my office; sleep was out of the question. I sat down at the computer and detailed Bob's fourteen years of education, his awards, achievements, academic research, and UCLA teaching position. He was only 66.

I called Cindy, who relayed the information to Kathy, who sent it in to the *L.A. Times* and the Montana newspapers.

The funeral was to take place on the exact day Hilly and I were scheduled to leave for China. Instead of traveling with him to Beijing, I flew into the small Missoula, Montana airport, planning to meet him three or four days later to take up the tour.

My sons, Brad and Glendon, were waiting for me in their rental car when I arrived. We drove to Hamilton through the grassy flatlands at the mountainous base, smelling the pines. I marveled at the azure sky, a great contrast to the bustling city I'd just left. Bob's neighbor graciously offered his home to us, so we convened there. We all shared what we were doing. Even though we talked often on the phone, and I saw them individually, being together was special. I felt like the mother again; only now they were grown with lives of their own, no longer needing me. Instead, I needed them. The only one missing was Bob. He would have loved to be with us, all together.

Glen told us about the new furniture, solar power systems, and home he was designing in the Sedona factory he built. Cynthia relayed news of her anchoring job with CBS in Atlanta, and Brad, with his wife Tina, in from L.A., were both enthusiastic about their daughters and plans for his Internet networking business. I had missed them so much these past few years. We sat in a state of mourning for the loss of their father and my husband of 21 years. Now that he was no longer with us, all the negative feelings I felt so many years ago seemed to have disappeared. In death, I lionized him.

The funeral parlor was of gray stone, surrounded by pine trees beside a rolling stream. The children and I sat quietly on mahogany pews as organ music filled the chapel. I wanted to tell everyone present about this lovely, bright man, an accomplished surgeon and gynecologist, about his humble beginnings in Long Beach, California, working as a commercial fisherman on weekends to pay for college. No one knew him like I knew him. But Kathy insisted I not speak. These were her friends, and she did not want to share the limelight of being Mrs. Robert Good. I mourned our loss silently, honoring her wish. I was the outsider, the unwanted mourner.

The July sun sparkled through the stained glass windows, reminding me of my father calling upstairs to me, where we had similar windows, when we were 21, and Bob had arrived for a date. "Elaine, your breath of sunshine is here." He was, indeed, the bright, young, shiny-faced handsome fellow, full of hope, wanting to heal the world.

My boys spoke at the service. They talked of strange things I knew nothing about, such as the red good-luck shorts Bob wore when he fished. After the service, everyone attending was invited back to Kathy and Bob's home. The children and I drove together. Turning into the drive, we saw the house, built of logs, in a pasture on a lake, with horses in the front yard. *Oh dear,* I thought. *This is what he wanted, the mountainous backdrop, grassy fields, streams and lakes stocked with fish, away from the demanding patients and superficiality of Los Angeles that I knew always grated on him.*

As we walked toward the house, Kathy's bulbous, 97-year-old mother stood, belligerent in her floral peach house dress, spreading her arms akimbo, blocking our entrance. "Stay away," she said to me, "you're not invited."

The children stood firm: "The funeral is for our father, and we're not coming in without our mother."

With my daughter holding my hand, we walked in amongst the guests. I recognized a few, but most were Hamilton neighbors, or from Kathy's dour Idaho family. The pine dining room table was laden with cakes and cookies neighbors had brought. We nibbled on ham, potato salad and coleslaw, a stark contrast to the shivahs of my milieu. I sat outside in the sunshine with the few people I knew, counting the minutes until we could escape.

Bob had been a great admirer of Ernest Hemingway. He had not known him personally, but read and treasured his books, felt a kinship with the man, and had mourned his death. He talked about it for weeks. They had in common their love of Cuba and Hawaii; they read the same authors, were hard drinkers and devout fishermen. Both were clinically depressed before taking their lives. Bob could not breathe and was in constant pain so I understood. Bob mimicked Hemingway even in suicide.

The suicide was kept a secret until after the funeral. My heart was heavy, and a painful sadness overwhelmed me. Knowing Bob, the immaculate surgeon, he did the bloody act in the driveway so as to not stain the house. He used the same twelve-gauge shotgun I had hidden forty years before in the window seat of my art studio in Brentwood, California, anticipating this very event.

The Beijing skies were gray with rain lightly falling as my plane landed. Hilly met me in the hotel lobby wearing his multi-pocketed, tan touring vest, filled with maps hanging out; a big smile on his face, and welcoming arms. He had never been on a tour before and could not wait to share every moment of the past few days.

The next morning, with sun streaming into the blue bus, we toured through the crowded, hazy streets of Beijing. We caught glimpses of blackened trees, laden with soot, the early morning tai chi and qi gong groups in the parks and plazas, then drove on to Badaling and the Great Wall of China. Our group of twenty hopped out and marched en masse toward the entrance. I had to push myself to keep up. I could hardly move.

Going so abruptly from the suicide and funeral to the joyous experience of trekking the Great Wall of China, arm in arm with my beloved, was contrary to my mood. I attempted to feign lightness and stroll with Hilly but could not erase the horror of what I had left 24 hours before. I wore white jeans and a straw hat and found a place to sit on a substantial rock, high enough to see an expanse of the wall and watch my sweetheart trot along like a gazelle in his pocketed vest and gray beard, braving the Asian breeze. We had traveled so far to visit one of the seven wonders of the medieval world, from the Ming Dynasty, and there I was, paralyzed. All I could think about was Bob's death.

My original thought was, *Poor Bob. He must have been in horrific pain to commit such a violent act of self-destruction.* But then I got angry. How could he have inflicted such a vicious memory on his children? How would his actions affect their future? I knew that suicide ran in families. Would their father's act give them license to cut their own lives short if they were faced with what seemed to be insurmountable junctures? I was not sure they were tough enough.

I sat for hours on my rock overlooking the Great Wall, watching the tourists march along, depression and isolation gripping my gut. I asked myself: *Was Bob's suicide one last act of revenge for my leaving him? Did he intentionally want to sabotage my trip with Hilly?*

The Yangtze River was calm that morning as we motored in the small launch, the rising sun glistening on the water. Hilly stood at the bow of the boat, wanting to get the full expanse of the view as the wind lashed at him. I sat bundled up at the stern, nestled amongst the others, watching the dark hills come alive with green farms, goats, and peasants in brimmed hats working the land. On the tops of the hills we could see massive, boxy apartment buildings under construction to house the peasant-farmers once the river was dammed up. The deepening of the waters would allow large cargo to enter China. We felt fortunate to be witnessing the historical energy of the farms before they were erased from existence.

We flew on to Xi'an. Holding hands, Hilly and I descended the steps down, down to the below-ground dig, surrounded by darkness, that preserved the 8,000 terra cotta warriors and horses. Each one was individually sculpted, representing a different person. It was assumed that many depicted the 73 emperors who ruled for the thousand years that Xi'an was the capital of the dynasties. Hilly and I wandered through the amazing body of work in awe.

The burial ground, consisting of so much art, was an eye-opener, drawing me back to the reality of my own life as an artist. I realized we must tell our stories to let future generations know what our environment was like, what we felt and saw. To be there in the dark among such a discovery was a most enlightening experience. It proved to me that Bob was wrong when he said, "Why would you ever want to be an artist? That is what children do in kindergarten."

I felt a surge of life within me begging to re-emerge, inspiring me to return to my studio and produce work of value. I remembered what it felt like to be in my atelier creating any work of art, whether it was in oil, acrylic, or drawing; the mixing of the paints, the struggle to begin, the involvement, not letting go, and staying with it. The glory was in the making, not in the exhibition at the end. The creation itself was the reward. I could not wait to get home and go back to work.

CHAPTER

23

The Sanctuary

It was 2001, and the studio was like an old friend welcoming me back from the Far East as I faced the pile of canvas and stretcher bars sitting in the corner, beckoning. I could not bring myself to put them together or pick up a brush. Bob's death, and the long journey back from China had left me dried up. When I shared my plight with an artist down the hall, he told me about a maharishi in Brooklyn who helped him get through a blocked period. Intrigued by the idea, I made an appointment.

Wearing black over black, I took the subway to the distant reaches of Brooklyn, got out at Ditmas Avenue and walked six blocks, arriving at an old pink structure with potted boxwoods at the entrance. I rang the bell with trepidation. A thin, fair-skinned man with long white hair tied back, welcomed me in broken English. Inside, the odor of incense permeated the air. The guru was a rotund, dark-skinned man, with a shaved head, in a long white robe. With a gleam in his eyes, arms outstretched, he motioned for me to come in and sit down. Following instructions, I sat on a floor mat, cross-legged, in front of several large, shiny black rocks and a sea of illuminated white candles, his interpreter by my side.

After I relayed my plight, the maharishi chanted for thirty minutes while I sat with eyes closed, meditating. He spoke to me through his translator.

"Stop wearing so much black," he said. "White will allow light to enter into your life, and you should paint a small pyramid to stimulate your creativity."

"Where will I find a pyramid?" I asked.

"Look into your mind."

I looked up at him, eyes wide, shaking my head, thinking: *This is crazy, just too simplistic.*

As I arose to leave, he embraced me warmly. A powerful energy emanated from his aura, and I vowed once again to re-dedicate myself to my art. On the long subway ride back, I remembered the pyramids I had seen on my trip to Egypt several years back, although I had never thought to paint them.

Returning home, I did as he requested, spontaneously painting one small pyramid. Surprisingly, my creative juices did start flowing. I stretched twelve 17 by 17-inch canvases to document my Egyptian journey. Cheops at Giza was my favorite, the oldest and largest, built as a tomb for the Pharaoh Khufu. It was to be a testament to his life and the belief that the soul is reborn after death. The old photos from the trip became my research materials. I sketched onto the canvas with a brush, then mixed acrylic pigment with molding paste, marble dust and gloss medium, which I applied with a palette knife.

After painting the twelve small canvases, I stretched a 60 by 60-inch, and stroke by stroke, portrayed more details. I imagined myself there in the hot sun, struggling to pull up the stones with the bare-chested slaves. I ordered a large roll of canvas from Pearl Paint again, stretching and stapling directly to the wall, 10 feet high by 12 feet wide. I tied a house painting brush onto a long-handled basting implement, loaded my palette with the mixture and climbed the high ladder, step by step to the top, working feverishly to tapes of Gordon Jenkins' *Seven Dreams.* I worked from sunup to sundown until my right arm ached. Standing on a ladder had become my norm after years of drawing my *Cliff* series. I disregarded the doorbell and phone. As I worked, I thought of Kiefer, my mentor, whom I visualized on his ladder.

One day, several weeks into the series, the doorbell would not stop ringing. I climbed down in my paint-spattered sweats and opened the large double doors to the loading dock.

"Nassos," I said, surprised to see my elderly artist friend. "How good to see you. Come on in."

"I was in the neighborhood and couldn't pass without stopping."

"Don't know if I'm ready, but you'll see my new series."

We walked into the studio; the twelve small pyramids spread out on the floor, the 60 by 60-inch on the easel and the new 10 by 12-foot painting hanging on the wall, just begun. He sat down on the little black couch and with his seasoned eye, scrutinized the work. "Pyramids, why? You know no one will buy these."

"I'm not painting this body of work to sell. I am painting them because I need to document the majesty of the ancient pyramids. They're spiritual entities." I did not mention the Maharishi, certain he would not have understood.

"They do feel spiritual. It's good that you paint what you feel and wise not to focus on selling."

We often discussed our work with one another, sitting quietly in each other's studios. I was fortunate to have found a supportive friend of such stature with whom to share my thinking and work.

"You know, today's the first Saturday after Labor Day, the opening of the new art season, and there are lots of receptions tonight. Want to go? Castelli's showing Lichtenstein."

"I've been so immersed in my work; I forgot what day it was. Sure, let's go."

Hilly's music business kept him busy on Saturdays, so I often went to the galleries with other artists.

Nassos and I met two hours later at his studio on West Broadway and walked over to Castelli's building. Lichtenstein was in his glory again, showing his interior paintings with enlarged Ben-Day dot patterns.

Always curious about other artists' thought processes, I asked, "Tell me Roy, what was your inspiration for this series?"

"I couldn't think of what to paint. Then I opened up the yellow pages in the phone book and saw the furniture ads."

We went upstairs to Sonnabend, Leo's ex-wife's gallery which was showing Mel Bochner's number paintings. The new art season brought a frenetic energy. Artists were selling work on the street, and mobs were going from gallery to gallery. SoHo on Saturdays was wild, and we were part of the madness.

The orange sun on the Hudson River was setting, the days getting shorter. Nassos's vision declined as the light in the sky faded. He had dry macular degeneration, which had not been helped by injections. After the openings, I took his arm and guided him along West Broadway and into the dim, wood-paneled Broome Street Bar, the scent of beer permeating. We had sat at the same table in back by the window every week for the past twelve years.

Sonia, the Swedish waitress, said as she saw us come in, "The usual, tuna melt on pumpernickel toast with a dinner salad?" We laughed in unison.

"You know we'll never change."

After dinner I walked Nassos across the street to his loft and made sure the door was locked before I left.

It was warm and windy, always windy in September down by the water. I walked alone, passing the galleries, crossing Canal Street packed with designer knock-off shops, crawling with sidewalk vendors and throngs of bargaining tourists. Always a little frightened in that area, I raised my head and barreled through at a fast pace. Entering Tribeca, the manic energy of SoHo dissipated for me.

I sometimes forgot the city and could have been anywhere when I was up on my ladder with the music flowing. Hilly and I talked every morning and night when we were not together, so when the phone would not stop ringing during work hours, I didn't think it was him. This time, reluctantly, I climbed down and picked it up.

"I have a surprise . . . tickets to see *Tosca* at the Met," Hilly said.

"How did you know? *Tosca* is one of my favorite operas." And I thought: *He is my thoughtful angel, always bringing pleasure into my life.*

"I know you; that's how."

Hilly arrived, his big, bulky frame so handsome in a navy blue suit with a red striped tie. I was glad I had gotten myself together in a long black velvet skirt with a white lace top. In supreme splendor, we felt like the king and queen as we exited the cab at Lincoln Center. James Levine conducted, and Luciano Pavarotti sang, while Hilly reached for my hand and smiled into my eyes. There was no doubt that we were indeed soulmates and there could not have been a more magnificent evening.

Franco Zeffirelli's sets were inspirational. I became fixated on his vibrant, movable, elaborate backdrops, which were more creative than any art I had seen. I wrote him a long letter expressing my admiration and asked to work with him designing sets. I waited patiently for a reply, which never arrived.

I realized Hilly was right; I should enjoy New York instead of isolating myself in the studio. I continued to paint six to eight hours a day but set out to see and experience as much of New York City as possible. When guests were visiting from out of town, I took them to the Metropolitan Museum to listen to late afternoon string quartets playing Bach in the rotunda, as we sipped Merlot. Afterwards, we went up the elevator, as music wafted its walls, to the sculpture garden on the roof to see the Rodin sculpture, and watch the sun setting on the city and Central Park.

When they went back to their hotels, I made my way downtown on the east side to sit quietly with Hilly at CBGB's in the corner, holding hands while listening to his most recent musical find.

It was still September, a hot and muggy Sunday when Hilly said, "I have to get out, see some green. I really need fresh air."

"How about Central Park? The subway's fast and easy."

We grabbed *The Times* and our bottles of water and were there in minutes from Tribeca. It was like a full day of vacation, smelling the grass, lolling in the sun, dozing under a tree, and feasting on two-dollar hot dogs. By evening, we went back downtown and stopped to have dinner at a cafe in the glassed-in Winter Garden extension of the Trade Center as we watched the purple sunset on the Hudson, with New Jersey in the distance. This was surely the happiest, most productive period of my life.

The next evening, I walked over to my gym, Executive Fitness, on the top floor of the Marriott Hotel between the two World Trade Center towers. After working out, I swam a half-hour in my reserved lane at the pool. The water was cool as I stretched my arms in a side crawl, returning with the backstroke. Echoes from the lapping water resonated throughout the enormous space, with workout machines surrounding the pool like a studded belt. I made my way to the dressing room and took a hot shower. It was 9:30 p.m. I chatted with one of the girls who worked in the gym on the way down the elevator. She was preparing for the high jump in the Olympics. Making idle conversation, I said, "You working tomorrow?"

"Yessiree, got to get home to bed, I'm on the early shift."

"See you Wednesday," I said as we both dashed off into the night.

I changed elevators to go the rest of the way down, walking through the World Trade Center, Number Two lobby, to get to the plaza. On that Monday evening, a classical guitarist, Julian Bream, was performing to about 60 tourists and neighbors gathered on folding chairs to enjoy the perfume of the starlit summer night. I sat on the black granite ledge surrounding an old cherry tree, thinking, *I love this city; there are cultural gems hiding around every corner.* Then I walked down the long flight of stairs and up West Broadway, six minutes to my loft on Franklin Street.

CHAPTER

24

They Flew Down Like Giant Birds

It was a Tuesday, and the wind had died down. All was still, with the sun peeking out from the horizon. There had been a smattering of rain during the night and wisps of clouds hung low. Birds were chirping on the windowsill of my first-floor corner bedroom. I woke up early to prepare for an 8:30 meeting with a contractor. As I sat in the kitchen of my narrow loft under the glass skylight sipping tea and reading the news, I felt the building shake like an earthquake, or was it an explosion? It was 8:46 a.m. I dashed away from under the skylight, fearing the ceiling would explode. Just then the phone rang: it was Hilly.

"My daughter was on her way down to court on Second Avenue, and saw a plane fly into the Trade Center. See what's going on."

I ran to the front door, then outside on my loading dock to see neighbors had gathered to watch the nearby burning tower. We thought it was an accident.

"What a jerk; couldn't he see where he was going?" said some fellow on my step. We couldn't believe what was happening. Just then the second plane came barreling toward the towers . . . jamming, crashing forcibly into the other building, bursting into a red ball of fire.

"Oh my God, it wasn't an accident."

Someone yelled, "Suicide bombers!"

We stood packed together tightly against my building. I could hardly move or see out. I forced my way through the crowd to catch sight of the plane as smoke and flames filled the air. We stood there, silent in disbelief.

"Look! People are jumping out of the windows," someone said. I had to look twice. They were like giant birds diving straight toward the ground; frightened souls flying through the air as each floor burned down, down, level by level, their only hope for survival. Then the second tower imploded in a massive black plume of smoke, the building falling to its knees like a wounded soldier.

"Help!" shrieked the voices.

My next-door neighbor had recently adopted a five-year-old child from Costa Rica who was in one of the five schools near the Trade Center. He broke our silence screaming, "Sam, I have to get down and find Sam."

"I'll go with you and help the others get out," I said.

We ran west to the river, then down toward the Trade Center along the water's edge. As we arrived, we saw screaming children barreling out of the building with their teachers. I lost my neighbor in the frantic, racing crowd. Then at 10:28, tower number one imploded in an immense black cloud. I could not go forward, it was too dangerous. Hundreds of terrified people were stampeding away from the towers, toward me, to save their lives. Some had run down 50 to 100 flights. Secretaries in good suits carrying high heels, stock brokers in Hermes, attorneys and accountants with briefcases, storekeepers from the underground city, restaurant workers in aprons, janitors, hairdressers, all running from the collapsing towers for safety. Some fell down on the ground in relief, some in exhaustion.

"I'm alive." Many were sobbing, some were praying. The thick black smoke engulfed us all as white ash fell like snow.

I sat down on a bench to catch my breath saying to no one in particular, "This is a war."

Walking back to the loft amid the bewildered, injured and thankful, I spotted my neighbor walking with his arm around little Sam, his son. Thank God he found him alive. Sitting in my office facing Franklin Street, immobilized, I tried to reach my children. A sudden heavy pounding on my window startled me. It was the police.

"Get out of the building, fast!" I peeked out the front door and was immediately herded to the triangle at the juncture of West Broadway and Varick. Someone said there was a bomb threat. We all stood huddled together for thirty minutes, until the police told us to go back into our buildings.

By this time, it was 5:00 p.m. I remembered my 8:30 a.m. appointment that never showed and realized I had not eaten all day. I walked the nine blocks up West Broadway to Houston Street and sat at a small table outside the Silver Spurs cafe, watching the glowing towers burn from afar. I called Hilly, and he came to eat with me. As nightfall approached, we walked to my loft and began to realize that everything in sight was covered with ashes and smelled of smoke. It was desolate and dark, with no power, haunting and frightening. In the loft, we lit candles and carried them as we passed from room to room. Hilly and I were not living together; but on that night he stayed, and we held each other, thankful to be alive.

The World Trade Center was my neighborhood; it housed my bank and drugstore, my gym, my world. I treasured that azure-carpeted, spotless gym. The kids who worked there were my friends. And the eighteen-year-old African-American girl training for the Olympics. *Were they alive? Could they have gotten down from the top floor of the Marriott and then down the two elevators?*

The next morning as I showered, I replayed events from the previous day, touching my numb skin with my fingertips, questioning my existence. *I am here and they're not.* The sirens from ambulances rang out non-stop each time they found a body. Most were dead when found. Heavy trucks rumbled down Church Street empty, and back up West Broadway filled with wreckage, headed for the dump, loud and heavy on the road. My loft and office were between those two main arteries.

Donning a face mask and helmet, I rode my bike a few blocks down to see the cordoned off site at Chambers Street, the fire still burning. The air was like a thick peach soup; cars and every object around were covered with a creamy ash, destroyed. We were all stone-faced, still in shock. The landline phones were down and all the power out. I thanked God for my cell phone.

By nightfall I was drained and told Hilly not to come down, thinking I was fine and would just go to bed early. By dusk I was hungry and wanted to get something to eat. No place was open, no markets or restaurants, nothing. When darkness fell, it was a searing, silent ghost town with no one on the streets. A dead zone, "Ground Zero."

I started wandering, thinking: *Surely around the next corner some place would be open to get dinner*. I trekked east toward Chinatown, walked and walked until I found myself in the old East Broadway section. One tiny joint was open on a dark side street; it was mobbed, and no one spoke English, the menu all in Mandarin. Walking home in the dark, I got lost. Disoriented and frightened, the glow from the burning towers gave me a point of reference. At my loft, all electricity was still off; I stumbled through the dark space to my bedroom and fell into bed.

As the days passed, a charged panic prevailed. The suspense and frantic search to find the living before it was too late, heightened. The city was in deep mourning. At our firehouse on North Moore and at fences of other firehouses throughout the city, there were impromptu shrines with lit candles, flowers and photos of missing loved ones, pleading to be found. With the stench of death at my doorstep, the acrid dust invaded every nook and cranny of my home. I could feel the spirits of the dead souls.

Television crews parked in front of my loft day and night counting the number of dead, found and unfound. At first CNN reported 2,000, then 2,500, then it was "2,976 at last count." The skeletons of the Twin Towers continued to smolder. By day four, unrelenting sirens were still blaring as the stench increased from the unfound, rotting bodies. It was a silent, smoky graveyard. We were warned not to open our windows or use air conditioners. However, at the same time the EPA reported the air outside was "not harmful." Later, this was refuted when lung problems and cancers developed.

There were no subways, buses or cabs south of 14th Street. I was hungry and my cupboards were bare. Donning helmet and mask, I rode my bike up a deserted West Broadway to 14th Street, out of Ground Zero, locked it up on a light pole and got on the uptown subway, still operating from that point, exiting at 57th Street. As I walked up the stairs, I saw a girl licking an ice cream cone. I could not believe my eyes. We were in a war zone downtown, and uptown it was life as usual.

"Where did you get that ice cream cone?" I asked, as though I had been in the jungle for a year.

"Across the street in that deli," she said, pointing. I went in and bought ice cream and an apple, then made my way over to Central Park, lying down on the grass, staring at the pure blue sky, smelling clean air. People were sitting around reading, laughing and talking as if nothing had happened. I dozed off and awakened with a start. *I have to get home before dark.*

I took the subway down to 14th and went into the Food Emporium market to shop. Then I rode home with plastic bags full of food hanging from both handlebars. It was almost dark when I reached Canal Street. State troopers stopped me, demanding proof that I lived in Ground Zero. One officer personally escorted me the four blocks south to my loft, instructing me to stay inside.

The power had been returned, allowing me to escape to the bed and wicker sofa in my darkened bedroom, farthest from the noisy street. Unable to think or work, I picked up trashy novels, and for weeks I languished in my bedroom, reading and watching TV from my thirteen-inch Sony, while the sirens and rumbling continued day and night. On television I saw scenes filmed from my own corner. I left my loft only to survey the situation by bike, having no desire to run away as some did.

In the beginning the city would not allow cars to drive below Houston Street. Then, after several weeks, the restraint was lifted, allowing foot traffic only. Hordes of tourists came every day, filling the streets to gawk at the devastated site. The hardest hit apartments and lofts near the Trade Center, with doors and windows blasted open, were looted. Some of my neighbors moved uptown to good hotels with maid service, staying for months. Some moved permanently into The Chelsea. Other families left town, never to be seen again. Selling was out of the question. Our valuable lofts had become worthless.

The EPA sent a crew to clean the walls and floors of my loft, and the City paid us a nominal sum to stay, not wanting a mass evacuation. On several occasions, I was in my darkened bedroom reading when the doorbell rang. I opened the inside door, then the door to the street, and saw two middle-aged strangers looking up at me. "Can I help you?" I said.

"We're psychologists sent by the City to see how you're handling the trauma. Is there anything we can do for you?"

"That's very nice," I said. "No, thank you, I'm fine." How could I open up to a stranger on my doorstep? When they left, I ambled back to my bedroom, and crumpled in a heap on the bed.

Hawkers took advantage of the situation and started selling American flags and other patriotic kitsch on the street. I bought a six-foot American flag and taped it to the inside of my office window facing the street, thus declaring my patriotism. Robert De Niro started the Tribeca Film Festival to bring positive energy back to the area. Mayor Giuliani planned concerts and brought Paul Simon in to boost our spirits, proving to the terrorists that we had not been brought to our knees.

The stuffing had been kicked out of me and initially, I had no desire to go into my studio. When I finally walked in, the only subject I could bring myself to paint was to reiterate the disaster on canvas over and over. I painted people jumping out of windows, flying straight down, then painted over them with fire raging around them.

They were too painful to look at. In the middle of the night, I got up and, in my bathrobe, walked to the corner and dumped those canvases in the trash. I had to get rid of them.

Ultimately, I painted ten 34″ wide by 80″ high canvases in a pinkish yellow atmosphere, some with the dead souls subtly hovering beneath.

Eight or nine days after the disaster, all the landline phones were still out, but I could use my cell phone in some areas to keep in touch with my family.

"Yes, I'm alright, just shaken," I said to my daughter. "It's pretty grim, ashes and flesh-colored dust everywhere, with the smell of burning bodies."

"What can I do to help, Mom?"

"Come out to Long Island for my birthday in late September. My tenant will be gone by then. I think everyone else in the family will come. It'll be good to be together. I miss you guys so much."

After the San Andreas Fault earthquake in Los Angeles several years before when the Joan Rivers entourage escaped my home, I had one more tenant and then put that house on the market. When it finally sold, I bought a smaller house on a wide creek called Sam's in Bridgehampton on the eastern end of Long Island as income property to rent out in the summers. During the World Trade Center disaster, I had a tenant in that new house.

"I need to get you away from all this," Hilly said. "Let's pick out that rowboat you've been wanting, so when the kids come out, we'll be able to take them rowing on Sam's Creek."

"But I have a tenant in the house."

"We'll get a motel room. Come on, it'll be fun."

Driving was still off-limits in Ground Zero. Hilly double-parked on Church Street, just south of Canal. I walked with my suitcase and found him, climbed into the car and off we went as the Towers continued to burn. It was great to escape, but I could not leave it emotionally. On Old Montauk Highway in Westhampton Beach we found a boatyard, and as we looked at rowboats, I said, "What are we doing here?" It seemed almost sacrilegious, too much of a departure. With heavy hearts, we ordered a twelve-foot aluminum Lund rowboat with oars.

We found a motel in Southampton for two nights and, of all times, the smoke detector wired into the ceiling went off at 2:00 a.m. Hilly and I stood up on the bed, both jumping up and down, trying to disconnect it. When we finally yanked it out, we fell back to sleep, but I woke up in a cold sweat, screaming, unable to escape the wrath of Ground Zero. Driving back into the city, as we transferred onto the BQE from the Long Island

Expressway, we could see the skeletal towers against the smoky sky, still glowing; harsh reminders of the reality we left behind.

For weeks after 9/11, our evenings were spent attending memorial services. The black we wore to be fashionable now became our mourning attire. We could not escape the omnipresence of grief. Ministers, rabbis and priests came from every part of the country to pray for the souls of the newly deceased.

The burning embers made the air hot as I rode my bike down silent, ash-filled streets day after day, while firemen dug for bodies and hauled off debris. Back at my studio, in a trance-like state, I mixed the atmospheric colors of the fiery-sky and slashed into the canvas with a pallet knife, depicting scenes of the buried dead. Each raw painting seemed to be filled with ominous horror.

Many artists had applied to The New York Foundation for the Arts to rent cheap studios, made available in vacant spaces on high floors in the Twin Towers. Many of those artists actually lived there illegally and, during the disaster, were sleeping, unable to get down. The ones with studios who were not living in the Towers, lost their entire inventories.

Hilly still managed to plan his concerts and run the CBGB rock club, but it was quieter. Before the disaster, he always came to me bearing armloads of flowers, cleaning out his neighborhood Korean deli. After 9/11, he walked to my loft at the end of the day, wearing his black CBGB t-shirt, plopping his pile of books on the table next to my black couch in the studio and sat, watching me prime my canvas and struggle to produce something . . . anything. He eventually lay down to read and fell asleep. When he awoke, we walked along Franklin Street, over the cobblestones, west to the river and sat on an iron bench, holding hands. We gazed at New Jersey on the far shore and into the foreboding black Hudson, sloshing under the dock, not speaking until the orange ball of sun disappeared. Words were meaningless. Closeness was all that seemed to matter.

The art scene in SoHo and exhibitions were still happening, out of courtesy for fellow artists who had worked years for preplanned shows, but few came and those who did were dour. West Broadway had become empty and silent. All the frivolity had disappeared.

After my summer tenant left, Hilly and I drove again to Bridgehampton. We passed the burned-out forest on the south side of Sunrise Highway, then the Shinnecock Inlet, green trees and farms, streams and more trees. The sweet air and the purity of nature was healing. We stopped at a market and bought a large turkey with all the fixings. At the house, I found the old, rarely used, white lace cloth, and carefully spread it onto the extended table. We put out both the low and high white candles and from the garden cut red Rosa rugosa for the centerpiece.

The following day Hilly picked up Bradley and Tina at Kennedy Airport with their little girls Lance and Max. They had come from Los Angeles. I went to MacArthur Airport for Glen, who flew in from Sedona. Cynthia, Joey, and their two boys Alden and Julien, were on a plane from Atlanta that sat on the ground, delaying their take-off eight hours, fearing another attack.

At last we were all seated around our old shiny walnut table, each saying a prayer of thanks for our blessings. Seeing us all together made me think of Bob. He would have loved to see the children and grandchildren. Sitting at the head of the table, I stood up and sanctified the innocents who had lost their lives in the Towers, and suggested we add Bob to our prayers. The next day, Hilly and Glen gathered up the oars and rowed the children on the new boat down Sam's Creek and onto Mecox Bay. My heart was full, but still frightened.

My fears increased daily. *Should I continue taking subways and the 4:01 train out to Montauk and all points east from Penn Station on Fridays, when Hilly did not come?* It seemed obvious that the thousands congregating were an open invitation to terrorists.

CHAPTER

25

Vanished

On our next trip to Long Island, in the middle of the night, Hilly had an epiphany. I thought he was talking in his sleep, but he was awake.

"We need to get busy, be productive and work the land, build fencing around the trash cans." I rolled over and kissed him. He pulled me close and stroked my hair. The strength of his arms and warmth of his body calmed me. In the morning he elaborated his ideas, prancing around the bedroom, waving his arms.

"Let's get rid of all those ugly shrubs and weeds and order a truckload of top soil, to build up the land around the creek, so it won't continue to flood the yard when it rains."

As I brushed my teeth, I said, "You're right, we've done enough wallowing."

I opened an old phone book and, scanning the Yellow Pages, found a dirt contractor and ordered a load of topsoil. It was late September and the days were cooling.

For the next month, we wore old polo shirts, garden gloves, worn jeans and tore out wild brush. Some days we worked in the rain and, when the weather improved, with heavy rakes as we spread out the fresh black soil and scattered grass seed. Smelling of sweat and mud, exhausted, we left our muddy shoes outside the door at night, happy to find the rains had washed them clean by morning. At Home Depot we bought treated wood fencing, piling it in the back of Hilly's ample teal green SUV. He did most of the work, embedding the posts in cement and tirelessly pounding away, until the trash can enclosure was complete.

The nights had turned chilly enough to build a blazing fire. In our robes, while he practiced his guitar, I made soup from chicken, vegetables, and potatoes. After dinner, Hilly strummed a country blues melody he was composing for me, then played an old song that I knew, and we sang together. I never sang, except in the shower; surely God was shining his light upon me, to have this late life relationship, something I never imagined possible.

Over the next four years, the aftermath and terror of 9/11 faded. Hilly and I became more optimistic about life. The city was rebuilding. Real estate had become pricy in SoHo and the art scene, originally headed toward Tribeca, had shifted to Chelsea where large spaces were cheaper. I counted 600 galleries in Chelsea during its emerging appeal as the new place for New York's art scene. Nasso's dealer, Leo Castelli, died and his young Italian wife took over the gallery, moving it from SoHo to her apartment on the Upper East Side.

On many nights, I went to CBGB's and sat among the densely packed crowd, listening to the Ramones or the Talking Heads, getting high on secondhand pot floating about the club. Hilly always found me and we sat quietly, holding hands. His large frame, sweet soul, and low voice warmed my heart. I knew he wanted me there. One night he whispered in my ear, "Come on, I want to introduce you to the regulars."

Then, he dragged me around the club saying, "Hey gang, I want you to meet my sweetheart. This is Elaine." I walked around with a big grin plastered on my 64-year-old face, feeling like a queen. It was one big party every night for him. After years of packed houses, I understood why he loved coming to my tranquil, quiet painting studio.

And then on one special night in autumn, the leaves were falling, there was a chill in the air, and we were celebrating our two birthdays, one day apart. We walked hand in hand to a new Thai restaurant near my loft in Tribeca, and ate an exotic buffet amid candlelight and crystal chandeliers. Proudly wearing the alpaca sweater he had given me for my birthday, I noticed him glowing when he saw how much I loved it. We had been together nine years. During our dinner conversation, I casually suggested that we live together; he could move into my loft. An uneasy silence settled upon us. He seemed disturbed, changing from radiant to mournful, before my eyes.

Stammering, he turned away, and then said, "Got to get back to the club," and walked me home. The next day I telephoned and could not reach him. He always called several times a day.

Without a word, he withdrew into oblivion and vanished.

CHAPTER

26

I Found Your Treasures

I took the #1 train up to West 86th Street and walked to 87th and Broadway. Alexandra's office was in her small beige living room, decorated with hot pink pillows, on the sixth floor of an old landmark building. A highly recommended psychotherapist in her early 60's, she had straight gray hair and large, comforting blue eyes. She shook my hand, introduced herself, and I immediately felt at ease.

I had been asking myself: *What have I done or said to perpetrate Hilly's disappearance? Was there another woman?* I realized I had been critical of his yo-yo weight, worrying about his health, thinking, *it couldn't be that.* I said to her, "Perhaps we had become too close and he was frightened." She listened without saying much, but when I left, I knew I had a friend in whom I could confide.

I wanted to talk with Hilly, but his office assistant said he was away. I sequestered myself in my studio for weeks, and the isolation was like 9/11 all over again. I stoically wandered aimlessly, in and out of the galleries, ending up at the café across from CBGB's, staring at the club, wondering where he was. After talking to him many times a day, every day, coupled with the magnitude of our closeness, the loss was profound. Each time I entered my loft, I murmured, "Where are you Hilly? I miss you, I need you."

He had been more of a presence than anyone in my life, always there, on the phone, in person, or on my mind. His absence was a death, a shock to my system. I started bleeding internally and went to see my internist. He sent me to a gastroenterologist. I was very ill and had the beginning of ulcerative colitis.

In a desperate attempt to understand him better, I went to see his fragile, 95-year-old mother Bertha, at The Hallmark, her board and care facility in Battery Park City. She was waiting for me, dressed in a bright red blazer and blue slacks. In her low, raspy voice, she said, "Elaine, how wonderful to see you. I'm honored. You've come alone?"

She may have noticed the guilty expression on my face. I always had come with Hilly.

Bertha and I walked down the path from her building to the river and sat on a cement bench to rest. I told her what had happened, and quietly, in her low-pitched voice, she told me, "When Hilly was a child, he would run away when he could not live up to what was expected of him. At age eight he brought home his report card and, before we could see it, he hid in the cornfield, staying all night. We were frantic. He did this again and again. At sixteen, he disappeared for six months, hitchhiked from our New Jersey farm to Los Angeles, where he looked up your grandfather, my mother's half-brother, who called to let us know he was safe. By the time he returned home, my hair had lost its color."

Her resemblance to me was striking. The only difference was her thick white hair and more wrinkles.

After learning his history of disappearances, I had a better understanding of his secret ways, but it did not change my suffering. I could not sleep or eat and wondered if I could ever feel normal again. It did not dawn on me to ask a medical doctor for tranquilizers or sleeping pills. That was not in my lexicon in the 1990s. And, of course, I no longer could tolerate alcohol.

Two months after his disappearance, the doorbell rang and there he was, unannounced; not in his usual black T-shirt, but groomed in an ironed, long-sleeved, blue-checkered shirt, with his beard freshly trimmed.

I ushered him in and, stiffly, we sat on the brown leather sofa in my living room. With puffy eyes and heart pounding, I folded my arms into one another under my breasts, and was mute. His low voice was hesitant. Instead of being my sweet, loving soulmate, he had become a stranger. "I was in the neighborhood and thought I'd stop by and say hello."

Had I rushed to him and cried in his arms, telling him how I missed and loved him, and been soft and vulnerable, we might have come back together, but I sat as far away from him as possible, unconsciously being self-protective. I fidgeted and ran into the kitchen to get us water, handing it to him with an outstretched arm; paralyzed, speechless. We sat there in silence, both unable to express ourselves. He stayed no more than ten minutes.

Thank heaven, I had maintained my relationship with Nassos and other artists. In two months, I forced myself to get back into the artist's life. I rode my bike on Wednesday mornings through New York University's grounds to Violet's Cafe and sat at the round marble table in the corner with other artists. We jabbered about the art scene. I tried not to mention Hilly.

On Friday night, I walked to SOHO20 Gallery where the Artists Talk on Art group was meeting, and listened to Robert Long speak about his new book on Willem de Kooning, staying afterward to schmooze with the regulars. They asked me to be on the Board, and I accepted. The next day I called Nassos, and we met for dinner at the Broome Street Bar for our usual tuna melt on pumpernickel toast and sat in the back room. Then we walked around the corner and had our ice cream cones.

Nassos always inspired me and, seeing his wonderful studio,

I went back to my loft and sat in front of my work in the dark, then lit a candle and meditated. I decided it was time to focus on having another exhibition.

I made a list of all the dealers I knew and artist friends who had not seen my new work and spent the next few days calling to invite them to make studio visits. Among them was Elaine Housman, a sculptor. She had never seen any of my work and responded with gusto to my paintings and drawings.

"I think my dealer, Allen Sheppard, would flip for your work," she said. "Look at his gallery; it just opened in Chelsea on 25th Street. If you like, I'll call to introduce you."

Allen Sheppard was not a mainstream dealer, but he was credible; young and passionate about art and his new gallery. We had the same creative sensibility. I invited him to make a studio visit the following week. He came with his girlfriend, a dark-haired beauty dressed in yellow, a feng shui master. I walked with them around the studio, unrolling drawings, flipping through racks of large paintings, then the small, and going through flat files, showing the old silkscreen prints and photographs.

I sensed they wanted to talk privately and said, "Why don't you check out the basement storage racks and come back up to go over everything on your own." Then I tossed them the basement keys. "Here, take your time, I'll be in my office."

After about an hour, I heard their footsteps marching up the wooden stairs. They barged into my office, very excited and loudly exclaimed:

"We've found your treasures, your Erotic Series."

They were like two children having discovered chocolate for the first time.

"I couldn't exhibit that work," I said. "I've hidden those paintings for twenty years. In Los Angeles I was known for that genre, and don't want that image to stigmatize me here in New York."

"The work is amazing, it needs to be seen. It'll make a sensational show," Allen said.

I remembered that Hilly always declared my Erotic Series to be his favorite of all my work. I had dismissed him thinking, *my new work is more cultivated and advanced intellectually.* Now I realized that maybe he was not off course. Everyone can identify with sensual images. After thinking it over, I called Allen Sheppard and agreed to show the series.

We set the date and I began restoring paintings, damaged from shipping and years of storage. The plastic I used to protect them had, in some instances, stuck to the glossy surface and made them difficult to repair. These early paintings were in oil, easily damaged and more fragile than my new acrylics works. The restoration process necessitated my working in oil again. The smell and feel of the pigment, turpentine, and varnishes permeating my being brought back thoughts of my former life and painting in my Venice studio.

Sheppard was excited and put together a small brochure for which Donald Kuspit, the art critic, wrote an essay, excerpted here:

Marinoff's Erotic Series, again on display, is an important contribution to the post-conceptual revival of interest in bodily painting and esthetics. Each painting seems like a sensitive body in itself, built of layer upon layer of oil paint, each at once as delicate and flexible as tissue. The final result is a luminous image as smooth to the touch and emotionally evocative as skin. She has ingeniously translated the esthetic of the body into the immediacy of pain.

We put a full page ad in *Art in America* with one of the images, which attracted enthusiasm from buyers and other dealers. Invitations were printed with the same image and, while addressing it to collectors and friends, my strength returning, I decided to be bold and send one to Hilly. On it I wrote: *You were right about these paintings. They are my treasures.*

The night of the opening, the paintings were hung in the gleaming new gallery. Champagne corks popped, the lighting was perfect, and the crowd began arriving. Hilly appeared on the scene early, wearing the brown herringbone tweed jacket I had bought for him before we traveled once to Italy. I could not look him in the eye. With a smile on his bearded face, he chatted with Allen Sheppard and our old friends as though nothing had changed. Donald Kuspit came, surprising me by picking me up and twirling me around to congratulate me. Openings were always crazy, never what we anticipated, merely nights to be endured. I couldn't wait for the evening to be over. The best part of being an artist is the creation of the work, not the party at the end. A few friends came to my loft for a late supper of beef stew with sourdough rolls that I had prepared in advance. We sat around and were relaxed, a contrast to my previous after-opening dinners. I did not invite Hilly.

Allen Sheppard pursued Hilly to buy a painting, and the next week he called. "Hi, the show was great. How about dinner? I'm thinking of buying one of your paintings, and I need you to help me pick it out."

Over the nearly two years he had been away, my pain had turned to anger, and by that time, the last thing I wanted was to have dinner with him. He obviously was trying to worm his way back into my heart through my work. But when one has an exhibition, selling the show is paramount. Maybe I was masochistic; there was some secret part of me that still longed to be with him. My psychotherapist Alexandra begged me not to see him. I rationalized: *It's only dinner, Elaine. Go, get the sale for Sheppard, he needs to pay his bills.*

I told Hilly I would meet him at the gallery. When I arrived, he was already there, chatting with Sheppard. I helped him pick out a 48-inch x 60-inch painting he seemed to love. He had brought his big SUV, thinking he could purchase the painting and walk out with it. Disappointed when hearing he could not have it immediately, he was forced to wait three more weeks, until the exhibition closed.

"I hope we're on for dinner," he said. "We could go to your favorite place." I realized he was trying hard.

"Okay, we'll see if they have a table."

The skies burst open with a furious downpour as we approached La Lunchonette, on 18th Street and Tenth Avenue. With streaming wet hair and damp clothes, we barged in and were lucky to get our usual table by the window in back. At first, the conversation was strained. I was guarded and not in the mood for light talk, but we finally relaxed and started talking about our families and who was playing at Hilly's club. He began to call again, but I was reluctant.

A few weeks after the gallery opening, I had been to New Jersey to meet with a curator, planning another exhibition. While dozing on a public bus, on my way into Penn Station, my cell phone rang. It was Hilly.

"I'm in the emergency ward at New York Hospital. I need you. Could you come?"

CHAPTER

27

The Soul of an Artist

The clouds were dark and low; my head was in a haze as I flagged a cab. The cabbie plowed his way uptown through rush hour traffic to East 68th and York, the emergency entrance of New York Hospital. The driver pulled around the circle and I got out under the brown awning and walked to the reception desk.

"Hilly Kristal, where is he?"

The young girl flung her slim, dark arm behind her, pointing. "You'll find him around the bend."

It took me several minutes to focus on the harried scene of gurneys in the hallways, each with a patient, some moaning; some just waiting to be seen. The stifling odor of rubbing alcohol permeated the pale green room under fluorescent tube lights. I walked quickly past the gray, curtained-off areas, peeking into each. As I reached the far rear corner, I saw Hilly in the corridor, covered with a sheet, his eyes closed, with an oxygen mask covering his nose and mouth. I stood there for a few moments, then bent down and kissed his forehead. His eyes opened, he blinked twice, then reached out and grabbed my hand.

"What happened?" I asked.

He pulled his mask down, "I was taking my morning run. Suddenly I couldn't breathe; pressure in my chest, then so much pain. I got home and called my internist. 'Get to emergency as fast as you can,' he said, 'I'll meet you there.'"

"Put the mask back on, we'll talk later," I said, and walked over to the nurse's station. "What's going on with Mr. Kristal? Why is he still in the hall?"

"The rooms are all full," she said. "He has to stay here until one's available. Clogged artery. Doctor's upstairs with the cardiologist, setting up the procedure."

My months of pain and anger disappeared at the sight of Hilly, so vulnerable on that gurney. Bending down, I gently put my arms around him. "Sweetheart, you'll be fine."

I pulled over a stool and sat, holding his hand. An hour later the cardiologist came in wearing green scrubs, with an attendant. They wheeled his gurney upstairs to the O.R. as I tagged behind.

Since I had known Hilly, he had not smoked, but he told me that he did for forty years, plus all the secondhand smoke circulating the club must have had its effect on him. Living alone, he ate the club food kids working for him brought, usually at his desk, while running the club. He was big and strong, a tough guy, and he thought, indestructible.

I encouraged him to get out and exercise, dragged him to my gym at the World Trade Center, where he tried all the machines and ran the track. He felt good and started running on his own, even joined a gym in his East Village neighborhood. I was so proud of him. He had lost a little weight and seemed to be getting healthier. One day I had said, "How's the gym going? Makes you feel great, doesn't it?"

"I haven't been going."

"Why not?"

"I hate the crowds and smells, it's never convenient. I joined; what more do you want?" Then he said, "Running by the East

River, watching the leaves change and bridges silhouetted against the sky, reflected on the water, makes more sense to me."

After that I shut up. *He had the soul of an artist; running was the best . . . he was no fool.*

They inserted three stents, and Hilly went back to work in several days; he seemed to be thriving. Our relationship accelerated to a new level. I made a pact with myself never to ask for anything he was hesitant about. I did not need to live with him to be happy; I was fine on my own and realized that my independence was one of the things he loved about me.

Through all his years running CBGB, he was proud of the fact that the money taken at the door went directly to the musicians performing. The club's only earnings were from the bar. Consequently, Hilly never earned much and lived in a small walk-up in the East Village. In the past two years, he had started a line of clothing, which took off brilliantly. In the months we were apart, he sold the small Franklin Lakes, New Jersey condo he had bought to give us a place out of the city to run to when I had a tenant on Long Island and purchased a home on the Jersey Shore in Asbury Park.

"You have to come out with me to see my new place, help me hang your masterpiece," he said. I was reluctant and discussed it with Alexandra. "Absolutely do not go," she told me. "You're asking for trouble."

But I succumbed, intrigued by his need to prove something to me, and of course I wanted to be with him.

It was a sun-drenched Saturday afternoon when we set off for Asbury Park. On our way we drove through the main street of Hightstown before he veered off onto a side road and stopped in front of a small, old farmhouse. There were chickens running around in a large wire enclosure on one side and a vast cornfield in back. He got out a bottle of Poland Spring water, took a swig and turned to me with a blank expression. "This is it," he said, "the farm where I grew up."

The new three-story house in Asbury Park was the essence of Hilly: tall and strong, old and charming, with stained glass windows and dark wood paneling; his first real home. He had furnished it himself, with the help of Crate & Barrel. It smelled of fresh paint and new rugs. From the third floor we could see the ocean. We walked along the nearby channel to the rugged beach, a startling contrast to the small, placid lakeside condo he had sold. He glowed with pride.

I had come to conclusions about my own living arrangements while Hilly seemed to be out of my life. The stock market had plummeted and my portfolio was frighteningly down. The climate in the proximity of the World Trade Center continued to be dark and foreboding. No one smiled; there was no lightness of being. I needed to cross Canal Street with its hawkers, trash and rancid smells to get anywhere. And the infighting at my all-artists co-op had reached a point of total negativity. It was a typical New York art loft story. Alone and fragile, without Hilly by my side, the angry environment seemed intensified. My painting had stopped. After all my years of focus, nothing was coming out.

When I arrived at my home on the East End of Long Island, I felt buoyant, serene and at peace. The country air, as I exited the train, was like perfume to my senses. My friends there were bright, creative souls who also treasured the purity of the light, the farms and waterways. It was a jewel in my hands, to be nurtured and enjoyed and not wasted. I realized life was fleeting; why not be in the most desirable place on earth?

My daughter often said, "Mom, you can live anywhere. Why don't you go to the south of France?"

"Cynthia, I've found the south of France right here, only it's better, they speak my language."

I made the decision to put the Tribeca loft on the market and sell.

One Friday afternoon, Hilly and I packed the car like old times, stopped on the way to buy fresh fish and vegetables on Canal Street, then raced east to exit 70 of the LIE, where we stopped for a quick chicken salad sandwich. We wanted to arrive before dark so we could check the ocean, see if it was still there, our ritual. In the summer we sat on the sole bench at the beach, watching sunsets, marveling at the pinks and purples. But now it was cool, and we only stopped for a peek, saying to each other, "Yep, it's still here." At the house, we grabbed logs from the woodpile and built a blazing fire to warm the house.

We listened to the crashing waves that night and sat mesmerized by the view of Sam's Creek the next day. Hilly always brought two guitars, and the living room was a jumble of the weekend *Times*, my books and paintings; a mess to any outsider, but to us, a comfort. It was our special hideaway. It had been three years since his stents were inserted, and we had been walking a rapid three miles each weekend day as part of our regimen to keep his heart strong. On that day we were down to one slow mile, his gait more and more labored.

I begged him the next day, "Come on, let's do our walk, the doctor says it's important."

"Today is not a good day; I think I'll stay in."

I came back an hour later and he was asleep on the couch. I didn't want to upset him, but casually asked, "Feeling all right? Had the stents checked lately?"

"Don't bother me, I'm fine."

But I could tell he was not. In the middle of the night I had been awakened by his restless moans. Fatigued most of the time, he seemed depressed and could hardly get out of bed. When we got back to the city, he went to his internist for blood work and a check-up.

It was finally spring, a warm 62 degrees in the city, and I was working in my studio again, at last. The doorbell rang; it was Hilly, unannounced, direct from the doctor, his anguished face paler than usual. I embraced him at the door and he crumpled, right there in my arms.

Pulling him over to the couch, I said, "Tell me, what did the blood tests show? Did you talk with the doctor?"

Hesitant and confused, he blurted out, "I have lung cancer. Have to go in for more tests. There's a slight chance he's wrong, but the way I've been feeling . . . can hardly breathe, I know he's right."

He lay with his head on my lap, both of us speechless.

"Maybe you should get a second opinion?"

"No, the blood tests were pretty conclusive," he said.

I thought: *Where do we go from here?*

"Don't worry sweetheart," I said. "We'll do everything possible to get you well. You're strong; I know you can beat this."

He continued to go for tests at New York Hospital, stopping after each testing to share his results with me. "It's good to be here, to get away from the hospital and all the problems at the club," he said.

"What problems at the club?"

"We rent the club's space from the city, and they're aggressively trying to get us out. The eviction has been preying on my mind. I'm interviewing buyers, some from Las Vegas. Wanna go? It might be fun."

Sick as he was, we flew to Las Vegas and met with potential investors, going from one large hall to the other. Hilly loved the slot machines and played long into the night as I slept in the hotel room. Around midnight, he woke me up excitedly to tell me he had won $500.

On a warm August day during that period, when he still felt fairly well, we had gone out to Hilly's new house in Asbury Park and were invited to the home of another potential buyer in a neighboring town called Deal. The ten-foot black door was answered by a Chinese house manager who ushered us in through the well-groomed house, and out to the draped pool cabana. The father, son, and a striking, dark-haired woman in a long silver wrap skirt over a bikini were sipping cocktails, while two children swam in the blue tiled pool.

The two men rushed over, excitedly shaking Hilly's hand, as the house manager brought out a large tray of crudités. "Hope you brought your bathing suit."

"Sure did," Hilly said, as he slipped off his jeans, CBGB shirt, and immediately dove in. When he came up for air, wrapped in their plush, green-striped towel, the two men proceeded to hustle Hilly into selling them the club.

"We'll make it even better, clean it up, get famous rock bands to perform. You'll see."

Of course, it was exactly the opposite of what Hilly always intended for the club. He only wanted young musicians who wrote their own music, to keep it low-profile, not glitzy. While driving back to his place, Hilly stopped the car as we rounded the corner, slapped his hands on his head and said, "It just hit me, those guys are Mafia."

As we were climbing into bed that night the phone rang. It was 11:00 p.m.

"Hello? Oh hi, Lisa, what's up?" He listened for a minute then said, "Can we talk in the morning?"

His daughter Lisa had developed the habit of calling every night before bed as a child and continued into adulthood. That was sweet for a child, but she was 52 and an imposing woman with a law degree, usually bringing up stressful problems at that hour, and that night it was the eviction. Hilly became stressed and couldn't sleep. Sometimes when the phone rang, we would say: "There she goes again; sounds like Lisa's ring, should we answer it or not?"

CBGB's eviction was final. Hilly and his staff sold off some furnishings, packed up, and put the rest in storage, closing the world-famous rock club forever. They opened a small store on East 8th Street where they sold the complete line of clothing, plus shower curtains, jackets and hats. I took the subway down to the store. Soft rock was playing on the sound system, and there were posters from the club on the walls. The racks were shiny, coated steel. The jackets and shirts were all new, neatly arranged by size and color. It looked like a regular clothing store, only every item had the CBGB logo imprinted. I looked around for the boss and found him in the back, sitting at his desk, looking defeated and shabby, wearing his usual black CBGB shirt. But now his skin was sallow, eyes puffy and his beard needed a trim. He looked up, surprised to see me.

"Hi, you came to see the place; what do you think?"

"It's lovely, think I'll buy some shirts for the kids."

"Lovely like hell. It's the pits! A goddamn shirt store. Thirty-five years and this is all I have to show? Makes me sick."

"Sweetheart, you *are* sick."

He stopped, and with his whole body shaking, in his very low voice said, "I know. Next week they're opening me up to look around, see exactly where the cancer is."

Lisa was there when I arrived. Her slight, mild-mannered Dutch husband, Gerrit, and Hilly's curvaceous young brunette assistant, Louise, came an hour later. The four of us sat in silence on the green vinyl chairs outside the operating room. After an hour, the oncologist came out in his scrubs, beads of sweat seeping through his cap.

"Hilly's cancer is aggressive, definitely in his lungs, and I can see it has begun to spread. We'll put him on a chemo regimen as soon as he is up to it."

"I wanna see him," Lisa said.

"He's not awake, come back tomorrow. He'll be groggy when he wakes up."

Then she shouted, "Gotta see him!" Other families turned their heads. Her face was stern. "I'll wait. You guys go on home."

It was November when Hilly was discharged from the hospital. A series of chemo treatments was ordered. For the first one, I rode a cab to his store where he waited, then sat with him, reading in the crowded waiting room, drinking from the hospital's coffee machine. Later I delivered him to his apartment amidst a drenching downpour.

"It was a piece of cake," he said. "I feel fine."

The crash came a few days later, but it gave him an excuse to stay in bed and read. He never complained. Hilly had studied opera after high school instead of going to college but was street-smart and a voracious reader. His library overshadowed that of many a Harvard PhD.

On New Years Eve, 2006, he was between treatments and felt pretty good. We were at my house on Long Island and went to the movies, then home, curling up in our robes by the fire with hot soup. He insisted on sleeping in the guest room so he would not wake me. As I sat in our favorite chair alone, I noticed 32 prescription bottles on the table next to the chair, waiting for him. The ominous fear of his imminent death clawed at me.

Hilly's internist Dr. Francis Perrone had seen him through the stents, and they had developed a mutual admiration. Perrone was determined to keep him alive. After the chemo, Hilly repeatedly went to Perrone's office for B-12 injections and blood transfusions. He looked hardy after each procedure. It was after one of these treatments that we drove again out to be among the trees and farms near the ocean. The day was golden. Winter had turned into spring; the daffodils and tulips were blooming, with birds singing in my blossoming cherry trees.

He understood that the farms on the North Fork were similar to those he grew up with in Hightstown. So, for an easy outing, we took a drive to see the area. He was a farmer at heart and reveled in the visions and smells of the cows, chickens, and the magical beauty of the vast working farms. On the way back, I saw a quaint little cafe in Greenport where we stopped for a cup of tea and a sweet. I parked the car and started to walk in when I noticed Hilly leaning against the car, starting to fall, and then crumpling to the ground. I ran over and helped pick up his substantial body and put him back in the car. I rolled the seat back so he could lie flat and, back home, I helped him up the steps into bed. After wiping his brow with a warm cloth, I lay next to him and surrounded his girth with my arms until he dozed.

The next morning, the sun shone and he seemed revived. With his cane on one side and me on the other, we walked very slowly down the lonely road to the beach, peering at empty houses through winter hedges. We sat down, watching dogs running by their masters' sides and flocks of birds trailing gracefully through cumulus clouds while we listened to the crashing waves and smelled the salted sea.

CHAPTER

28

Tethered

My loft languished on the market for three years until suddenly, in 2006, my real estate broker had an offer and as soon as we started negotiating, another came in. I made a quick decision to go ahead with the highest bid, and before I knew what hit me, the contract was signed and I was locked into the sale.

Hilly had a daughter, son, and an ex-wife who cared about him and lived nearby, so I was sure he would be looked after during the next couple of weeks while I packed my living area, studio, and basement storage. Hundreds of paintings and drawings had to be wrapped.

Faced with no place in the city and my sweetheart so sick, I bought an apartment near the hospital on East 70th Street. It was a quiet area I had always loved and a total contrast to SoHo and Tribeca. The two-bedroom space was owned by the absent French Consulate, and available for immediate occupancy. I thought I could walk to see Hilly when he was in the hospital, or he could stay with me in the new place, even though it needed fixing.

I had not heard from Hilly for several days after we returned from the beach and called New York Hospital. Hilly had checked in. I rushed off to be with him.

"Hilly Kristal; what room, which direction?"

"Sixth floor, south wing of the Annenberg Building," the receptionist said, pointing. I rode up the packed elevator that smelled of body heat and disinfectant, arriving apprehensively, searching for his room amid nurses scurrying about.

I located it at the far end of a long hallway and walked in to see Hilly reclining in bed in his cotton print hospital gown, appearing healthy, his beard neatly groomed, looking handsome and smiling. A gorgeous woman with short blond hair, younger than me, whom I had never met before, sat in the corner chair next to his bed. She was ordering the nurse around as though she were his wife. I greeted him with a warm kiss.

He turned away intimating, *not now.*

I was shocked. *Who was this woman?*

Neither of them spoke. She was statuesque and voluptuous, wearing a stylish beige suit, high heels, and gold jewelry. I felt small and insignificant in my black turtleneck, jeans, and flat shoes. The blood rushed from my face and I could feel my jaw drop. After several minutes, I nervously made my way over to her and introduced myself.

"I know who you are," she said in a low, husky voice. "I'm Wendy,"

There were no other chairs in the room, so I stood. Hilly said, "I was feeling lousy, lost my balance, and Wendy insisted we call 911. They're doing more tests."

A long silence ensued. Perplexed and feeling intrusive, I said, "Hope you feel better," and walked out.

Where did she come from? Somberly, I sat on the iron bench by the entrance, unable to move, and then took the subway back downtown to continue my packing.

The following week, I moved everything out of my loft into the new apartment, putting most of my belongings in storage and the paintings in a Southampton commercial space. The few possessions I brought were piled high in the center of the barren apartment, which needed renovation.

In the midst of my chaos, Hilly started calling again. That old pain in the pit of my stomach returned. "Hi. I'm out of the hospital."

"Where are you?" I said.

"I'm at Wendy's apartment, the Upper West Side."

"Why are you there? Who is she?"

"I had to have someplace to stay. Couldn't stay in my crash pad; it's ice cold and I'm too sick to stay alone. Lisa told me, "You need to eat and stay warm."

"Why are you with her, and not with me or Lisa?"

"You were packing and moving, and Lisa doesn't have room in her tiny place with Gerrit and the kids."

How awful. Had I known, I would have rented a temporary apartment or held off on the move, but no one had said a word to me. "Who is that woman, Wendy?"

"She's an old girlfriend from 30 years ago when we performed at Radio City Music Hall. She was a Rockette. Lisa's stayed friendly with her all these years, and asked Wendy if I could stay at her place. I'm on her couch."

There was nothing I could do. My sale came at the worst time. I commiserated with his needs. When I wanted us to have a total relationship, being there for each other was what I had in mind. I had disappointed him and myself as well.

Two months went by. He was in and out of the hospital several more times, but after he went for treatments, he came by my new apartment near the hospital. I noticed his face had lost its color and his clothes seemed to hang on his big frame. He was becoming weaker.

By the middle of May, I was outside, painting the doorframe to the apartment terrace, wearing tattered jeans and Hilly's old red striped shirt. The phone rang; it was Louise, his assistant. "I'm at the hospital. Come over as soon as you can; he's taken a turn for the worse."

I ran the three blocks and took the stairs instead of waiting for the elevator and burst in. The pale green room overlooked the East River and Roosevelt Island, lost on Hilly who was on oxygen, his skin sallow, eyes alternately closing and opening. A larger than usual crowd was jammed into his small room: Louise, Lisa and her husband with the two grandchildren, plus three young guys from the club, and a nurse monitoring the heart machine. Hilly was oblivious to the commotion. Louise must have called everyone she thought would want to pay last respects. The doctor came in and shooed us all out, then transferred Hilly into intensive care.

When I came the next day, he was heavily sedated. Louise and Lisa were there, and we were instructed to put on masks, gloves, and gowns. In her commanding voice, Lisa let us know that she had power of attorney, and that from now on she would be in charge.

When Hilly became lucid, she asked him to make a list of everyone he would like to come visit, typed it up, and posted it at the nurse's station. Louise, from the club, came to see him the next day and left in tears. "I'm not on the list; they won't let me in," she said. I never saw the list, went almost every day, and the only person I ever encountered was his daughter, Lisa. After that first visit, I never saw Wendy again at the hospital.

It was the end of May and he had been in a coma for days. The heart monitor was permanently hooked up, and a feeding tube was inserted directly into his stomach. They put him on oxygen and inserted a catheter. After that, his kidneys malfunctioned, and they put him on dialysis, strapping his hands to the bedposts so he would not pull out his tubes. When he woke up after that, he became combative and deranged, swearing the hospital staff was out to get him. He frantically fought the restraints.

The next day when I came onto the floor, the nurse at the counter reported what had happened.

"Is Mr. Kristal awake?"

"I'm not sure, but go on in, you're on the list."

I put on the gloves, mask, and gown. He could not talk but motioned with his glaring eyes for me to come over. The nurse came to check the heart monitor and cleared the magazines off the chair next to the bed. When she left, I secretly untied one strapped hand closest to me, and held it. He was under sedation and did not pull away or try to take out the tubes.

He closed his eyes and after awhile I started singing: "There's a bright golden haze on the meadow . . . " His eyes flickered, and then closed. I sang, "Oh what a beautiful morning . . . " and then I just sat holding his hand in silence for a long, long time as he dozed. When I got up to leave, I gently tied his hand back to the bedpost, and kissed him on the forehead. His eyes opened wide and he surprised me by tilting his head back, kissing me on the lips and mouthing the words, "I love you."

That one action, those words, touched my heart so deeply, I drifted out, leaned against the wall in the hall so he could not see me, and sobbed uncontrollably.

Usually Lisa had already been with her father and left by the time I arrived, but I had gone to Long Island for three days, and when I returned, she was there. I paid my respects and left them alone. The next day, he was propped up in bed and seemed lucid when I walked in. I untied the restraint on one hand as I had before, and he immediately pulled out the trach tube.

"You're finally here; please, please stay with me." He looked deranged, eyes wandering, throat so sore he could hardly speak. "Goddammit, why won't they let me die? Being tied down is a living hell. I can't stand it."

He became combative and hysterical, pulling out all his other tubes. I tried to grab the restraints and put them back on, but he was still stronger than me. Climbing over the rails, up onto the bed, I grabbed his arms to hold him down and screamed for the nurse. "Help, somebody help!"

Two nurses rushed in. One took hold of his wrists firmly; the other tied his wrists back up to the side rails. I climbed down, collapsing on the chair, shaking with my head in my hands. *This is all so horrible. My poor sweetheart doesn't deserve this torture.*

The next time I came he was lying flat, doped to the hilt, and had developed pneumonia. They had inserted a permanent ventilator. He was delirious, eyes wandering, could not speak, and his restraints were tied on tighter. It would have been merciful to let him go.

The following week, they informed me that his cancer had spread to his brain. I sat with him mutely for hours each day, as he floated in and out of consciousness. It had been 60 days on full life support with his hands restrained. There was nothing I could do. Lisa had all the control. When I left his side, I asked the head nurse if there was someone I could talk with about Hilly. She had the social worker call me.

"I agree it's time to let him go, but we can't do anything," the social worker said. "Lisa has power of attorney, and Hilly did not leave a living will. She is a lawyer; we need to be very careful. She could sue the hospital if we removed any of the life supports."

I called Lisa to discuss the situation, not wanting to alienate her, because one word from her and I would be off the list.

"I have shared him with the world for 53 years, and now he's all mine," she said. "I intend to keep him alive as long as possible."

In my restless dreams, he pleaded with me, "Please let me go."

Day after day I went to see him in his mute state, sometimes not uttering a word, but most of the time I monologued everything we had done, all the places we had visited. I reiterated the story of the flight our ancestors braved from Christabel, in Ukraine, to safety in the United States.

Each night after I left, devastated by the torture he was enduring, my shoulders aching and head down, I searched for some new distraction. Spring had turned into summer. It was July and hot. I went often to Tasty Delight for a frozen yogurt and sat eating it on the bench outside the shop on Third Avenue and 72nd Street. Other times, I stopped at the hospital's gift shop and bought a tired hamburger, taking it to a neighborhood theater to eat for my dinner as I watched a movie. I hated going back to my apartment alone.

July turned into August, Hilly's hands still tethered to the iron railings, all life supports still intact. This big tough, humble, selfless man who spent his life championing young musicians with their careers, drug problems, and family issues was hopelessly hanging on to life by machines. In the past four months, his former large stature had diminished. His thick salt and pepper head and beard of wavy hair had thinned to balding and now were pure white. His life supports, with hands restrained, now numbered 86 days.

Somehow, his flowing in and out of consciousness became the norm, and I was the self-elected witness to the horror. In a courageous moment, I finally talked to Lisa. "I can't bear to see him suffer another minute; it's too painful to watch."

By the end of August 2007, it had been 90 days on life supports, restrained. Lisa must have heard my prayers because she finally called.

"I'm having my father transferred to Cabrini Medical Center Hospice on the Lower East Side tomorrow."

I waited a day, and then rode the Second Avenue bus down, the address clutched in my hand, searching for the building. I found the inconspicuous structure nestled between apartment houses. Inside, the walls were cheerfully painted orange, yellow, and green, with scenes of flowers and children in a field.

When I walked in, I saw that instead of tethering him to the rails, the hospice had placed large mitts on his hands to keep him from pulling out his tubes. This big, strong, amazing man, reduced now to a shadow of his former self, still had a presence. He could accomplish only one movement: he could put those mitts together and pull the sheet off his body. I arrived in that final room where he lay totally naked with nothing covering him. His legs were the circumference of my arms, and his head small with only wisps of white strands. I immediately grabbed the sheet from the floor and tossed it over him, kissed his forehead and sat by his side as his lifeless eyes stared straight ahead.

The following night, he was still in a medicated coma. I felt it was the end, though I had not spoken to Lisa since her call. I walked into the small chapel in the hospice and sat in a pew with a sense of finality. This was his 94th day on life supports and restraints. I was not a drinker, but unable to face my apartment alone that night, I discovered a darkened Brazilian bar on Lexington Avenue and sat staring into space for hours. Then, mildly drunk, I walked home in the warm dark of the August night.

The renovation of my new apartment at last was complete, and the following day the moving van arrived with my furniture. As they were bringing in the brown leather sofa Hilly had loved and sat in so often, Lisa called. "I asked them to remove the feeding tube yesterday and he just now passed away," she said. "I thought you would want to know."

CHAPTER

29

From the Memorials to my Cathedral

October 7, 2007, midnight at the 70th Street apartment: I was asleep when the buzzer from the desk in the lobby sounded. "Miz Good, visitor here," announced the voice. "Says you're expecting him."

Stumbling out of bed, I grabbed my robe and opened the door, just as Seyom Brown, Hilly's first and my distant cousin, emerged from the elevator. We sat in the dark as I told him about Hilly's long struggle on life supports. He had grown up with Hilly on the farm in Hightstown, and they were like brothers. Seyom was one of America's preeminent experts in international relations and world politics and had authored eleven books on the subject. His father, Benjamin Brown, was my grandfather's brother, the mastermind who brought our families to this country, found them jobs, and organized the farming community in Clarion, Utah. Seyom had flown in from Dallas for the first of Hilly's two memorials, this one for the family.

Early the next morning, the fall air was crisp as the cab sped down Second Avenue, passing the new subway construction and the traffic tie-up near the Midtown Tunnel amid horns honking, as the city was just waking up. Messenger boys on bikes were racing in and out of traffic as the whiff of fresh coffee emanated from open cafes and newsstand clerks untied bundles of morning papers.

❧

Lisa had secured a brightly lit hall in the YWHA on 14th Street, between First and Second Avenues. We were seated on folding chairs at round tables covered with green cloths. Deli platters covered the long table at the far end of the room. Photos of Hilly tacked to one wall showed him as a child with his mother, then as a teenager, and as a young adult singing at Radio City Music Hall. I saw only one photo at CBGB's, in his forties, but none as I had known him, in his sixties and seventies. I had so many and was sorry I had not thought to bring them.

I remembered most of the 35 to 40 relatives from stays at my grandparents' home as a child. They were a brilliant group, mostly doctors and psychiatrists. I had the feeling they considered Hilly to be the oddball in the family and doubted many had ever visited Hilly's club or seen him in years. They talked about him as a child on the farm and of their love for his mother, Bertha. It was as though the funeral was for her. Few knew the kindness of his soul and depth of what he had become.

Lisa had contacted several of the relatives to say a few words. I waited until all the others had spoken, then walked up to the podium and delivered my carefully prepared eulogy about the Hilly I knew. I noticed tears in some of the relatives' eyes. While standing, from the corner of my eye, sitting on the side, way back in the rear, I saw Wendy. A twinge of pain shot through me. *She's here.*

I paid my respects to Hilly's grandchildren, all the Brown families, and others I remembered, but I had no interest in light conversation. To me it was not a social occasion. I was the first to leave. The leaves were starting to fall in the breezy air that helped clear my mind. The high heels I wore were killing me and my gray summer suit was not warm enough to shield me from the torrent of wind that whipped up. Arriving at my apartment spent, I collapsed on the bed.

On October 18th at six o'clock, the sun was still shining on the lower East Side. The line waiting to enter the Bowery Ballroom on Delancey Street for Hilly's public memorial stretched to the corner and around the block. I walked to the front and, thankfully, the boy checking the guest list knew me. There were over a thousand young and old people waiting to pay their respects. They wore a variety of outfits, from conservative to punk; the patchwork of colors intensified in the glow of the setting sun. Each person had to be checked off as they entered. Thankfully, Lisa had invited my list of our mutual friends who I knew would want to come.

Inside, all was dim except for the spotlit stage. Patti Smith sang softly on the sound system. A large photo of Hilly in his forties, with curly auburn hair and a more recent oil painting of him on canvas as a gray-haired older man hung behind the mike. When all had been admitted and the ballroom was packed to capacity, the roar of chatter was deafening.

Lisa Kristal stood tall in a tailored blue suit, her dark hair neatly combed back, with shiny silver earrings. She tapped the mike, and all became silent. Her opening remarks were well prepared as she read from a script expounding on her heroic attempt to keep her father alive. She proceeded to introduce each speaker.

My close friends gathered around me as support. We concurred that this was Hilly's last great performance.

His music associates had their own special stories about how Hilly had saved or inspired their lives. The first was his attorney, Jason Swartz. "Hilly was uncommonly ethical, always available and determined to do the right thing."

"He never dismissed me, always listened, and tried to help get gigs," said a tall Hispanic musician, Juan Martinez, whose tattoo-covered arms were revealed by his sleeveless leather vest.

"He was the father we never had." Suzanne and Josephine, two cute young CBGB employees, wearing short skirts and high boots, spoke.

Amid cheers and clapping, the Ramone brothers appeared. "If it weren't for Hilly Kristal, we wouldn't have made it in the music world. He discovered, promoted, and took us on tour in his green van."

Debbie Harry, lead singer of Blondie, sang "Life is Beautiful."

I left my group, found an empty chair in a dark corner, took some deep breaths, then allowed myself to sob privately. I seemed like an anonymous bystander in their midst, and yet no one was as close to him as I was, after sharing our lives and bed for ten years. But Hilly was an icon to those from his music world.

I caught a whiff of marijuana in the steamy ballroom. By 9:30 p.m., many were still waiting in the long line to tell their stories as Charles and Irene, two artist friends, pulled at my sleeve.

"This is too much," Charles, said, "the place is stifling. It's crazy. Let's get out of here. It will go on for hours. They're turning Hilly into a saint."

"No, I should stay; I can't leave now."

"Come on, let's go eat." Charles said as he grabbed my hand and pulled me toward the door that Irene was already holding open.

Outside the dark ballroom, with my head in a swirl, we stepped onto Delancey Street, now quiet, the cold night air slapping me in the face. We walked arm in arm, Charles and Irene on either side, holding me up. It was the end of a long nightmare, but the memorial had warmed my heart. *Hilly would have been proud.*

A few blocks away we found my old favorite, Ray's on Prince Street, a tiny hole-in-the-wall Mafia joint across from my first apartment. We sat near the front, away from the shady characters clustered in the back, and gorged ourselves on manicotti and house wine.

I arranged the furniture and hung my paintings in the new apartment, then called my real estate broker, telling her to put it on the market for rent. The following week, suitcase in hand, I escaped to my oasis near the ocean in Bridgehampton.

After the three-hour ride, I stepped into silent emptiness. Before he went to the hospital, Hilly's guitars had lined the walls, and his pill bottles littered the old chest by our favorite chair. Now it was just a house, all cleaned up, Hilly's presence erased except for the photos of us together. The summer people had disappeared and the neighborhood was quiet. I sat for hours in our chair, remembering. I pulled myself up eventually, found my jogging shoes, and stepped out the side door, first walking, then running along the empty road to the sea. Plunking down on our bench, I reflected on my long journey: how I got to this place. I had so much and now a feeling of desolation overwhelmed me.

A squawking flock of geese in V formation returned me to the reality of the moment as they flew directly overhead. The air had cooled at the beach and I was chilled. Clouds blew in as the sun began to set, with oranges and pinks flooding the sky. I folded my arms, hugging my waist to stay warm, and ambled home, watching the lights start to twinkle in the windows along the way.

Arriving at my house, I saw two of my carpenters nailing shingles high up on the roof of the new art studio I was building. I stepped inside and John, my foreman, was locking up for the day.

"Good to see you home, Elaine. Your studio is turning into quite a cathedral."

"Wow," I said, glancing at the 24-foot ceiling and skylights. "You've followed my plans perfectly. I have a feeling the best work of my life will be produced here. Can't wait to get my paints out and start working again."

Epilogue

Fifty-seven years ago, I married a young medical student in Los Angeles. I had recently come back from studying fashion in Paris, where I stopped into the Louvre on my way back to my *pension* from school each day, captivated by the paintings. At 21, I realized that becoming a painter was what I wanted to do with my life. From that moment forward, I nurtured that fantasy. Along with raising my three children, art became my life. It saddened me that my husband never quite understood and therefore demeaned my passion. The women's movement gave me strength and courage to leave our 21-year marriage and pursue my own mission.

Moving to New York City was both exciting and frightening. In midlife, I had at last found my milieu. Each day when I awoke, I ran to the window to check the weather and see the action. I treasured the energy of the city and the changing seasons. I had to learn a new way of life. It was like living in a foreign country, a harder life, but somehow more rewarding. It was the highlight of my life and made me strong.

When the spring came and nature was alive with color and new growth, I took the subway up to Central Park, Nikon camera strapped over my shoulder, to document the flowering dogwoods, tulips and daffodils. Then the magnificent autumn with oranges, yellows and reds appeared. I collected leaves and sent them to friends back home those first few years:

"Can you believe what I see here in my new world?"

I was blessed to have been a part of SoHo's art scene at a fascinating time in American art history, to have dined with critics, entertained and shown with fine art dealers, and gained respect for my work. I proved to my former husband that being an artist was not a children's game.

In my need to support myself, I invested in the stock market and did construction and renovation. From the sale of the house I designed and built in Pacific Palisades, California, I bought other properties, designed new living spaces and built more. I know these projects took time away from my painting, but they were creative as well. They were my comfort zone, resulting in an income that allowed me to survive and thrive.

After selling my Tribeca loft, I was left with no studio in the city. Afraid I had cut off my ties to the New York art world I had waited a lifetime to create, I asked myself: *Why did I do that? Will I ever paint again, and if so, what will I paint?* My art always reflected what was going on at that specific time in my life. I refused to paint commercially just to sell. Dealers often dictated what colors or subjects they thought were in demand and I rebelled. *No one was going to tell me what to paint. Would I be able to create without collapsing cliffs, oil spill devastation, eroticism, or terrorist attacks?*

Throughout history, painting has been a reflection of the artist and the era in which her art was created. In his writings, Sigmund Freud talked about the visual artist as having poor mirroring in infancy. He wrote that the painter mirrored himself in his work. That is always what I have done. Significant works of art are often self-portraits, often so subtle as to not be easily detected.

Maybe now I can reflect the simple beauty of the magical light on the East End of Long Island, and the barren trees in spring silhouetted against a morning mist, or a glistening Sam's Creek reflecting the sky at sunset in the fall.

About the Author

Elaine Marinoff Good, 1934-2018, was born in Los Angeles, California. A fine arts graduate of U.C.L.A., she studied abroad at the Sorbonne in Paris. Marinoff is a critically acclaimed painter with over 100 exhibitions. In New York City her artwork was represented by Allen Sheppard and Andre Zarre galleries, and the Galerie Woeller-Paquet and das Bilderhaus in Frankfurt, Germany. She was adjunct professor of art at the University of California, Los Angeles from 1985 to 1988 and served on the board of directors of the Fine Arts Federation of New York City from 2002 to 2012.

Elaine Marinoff was an accomplished artist, but more than anything, it is her life that speaks the loudest. Refusing to be subjugated by the oppressive forces that bound most middle-class housewives of the 1960s and 70s, she fearlessly illuminated her deeper self, illustrating the profound desires of women everywhere. Critics, including Donald Kuspit and Robert Morgan, described her as "someone capable of transforming what she sees into a cataclysmic sense of reality."

Marinoff was not just a boundary-breaking artist; she was a passionate lover of life as well as of CBGB Club's founder Hilly Kristal, three children, and four grandchildren. Her artwork is cherished by hundreds of international collectors. In *Treasures,* she confronts social and artistic constraints of the time and shares her insights with unflinching candor.

Artwork by Elaine Marinoff may be viewed at
www.ElaineMarinoff.com

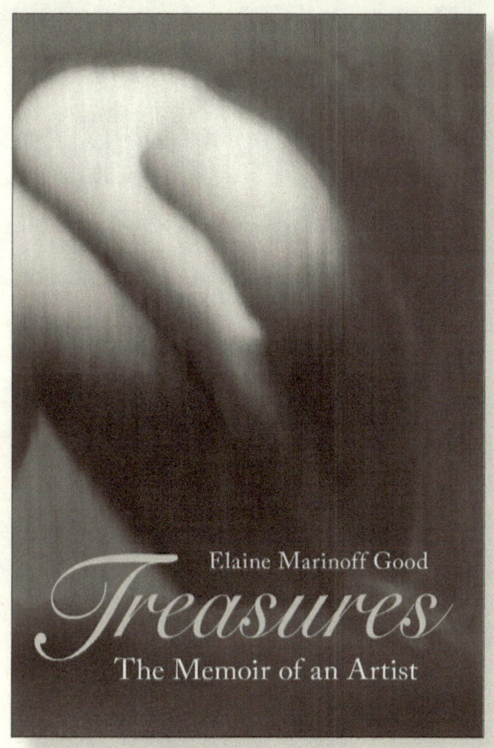

Treasures

The Memoir of An Artist

Elaine Marinoff Good

www.ingramcontent.com/pod-product-compliance
Lightning Source LLC
La Vergne TN
LVHW091051080826
845145LV00002B/707

* 9 7 8 1 7 3 2 7 9 3 3 3 0 *